101 Projects for BOTTLE CUTTERS

BOTTLE CUTTERS

Walter Ian Fischman

with designs by Chris Lewis
and Don Pope and photographs
by Mario Yglesia

THOMAS Y. CROWELL COMPANY/NEW YORK   Established 1834

Copyright © 1972 by Walter Ian Fischman

A Wentworth Enterprises Project

Photographs by Mario Yglesia, Black on White Studios, New York City

All rights reserved. Except for use in a review, the reproduction or utilization of this work in any form or by any electronic, mechanical, or other means, now known or hereafter invented, including xerography, photocopying, and recording, and in any information storage and retrieval system is forbidden without the written permission of the publisher. Published simultaneously in Canada by Fitzhenry & Whiteside Limited, Toronto.

Designed by Jill Schwartz

Manufactured in the United States of America
L.C. Card 72-82851
ISBN 0-690-59717-7
2 3 4 5 6 7 8 9 10

Contents

I An Introduction to Bottle Art / *1*

II Where to Get Bottles / *5*

III Types of Cutters and How to Use Them / *8*

IV Safety Precautions / *24*

V Types of Glass / *27*

VI Other Materials—Other Techniques / *29*

VII How to Make Money from Your Hobby / *34*

VIII A Gallery of Bottle-Art Projects / *39*

101 Projects for BOTTLE CUTTERS

I An Introduction to Bottle Art

You're about to become an artist, but don't let that frighten you. The new craft of bottle art is easy, as thousands of housewives, hobbyists, and home handymen have already discovered. The tools are inexpensive and the materials are almost free. The learning period is about ten minutes, and within a few days you can become an expert. Women who can't draw a straight line and men who smash their fingers when they try to drive a nail have become expert bottle artists. It's easy, it's inexpensive. You don't have to take a time-consuming course and you don't need any experience. Best of all, it's fun.

The material you'll be working with has a fascinating and romantic history. Glassmaking goes back almost six thousand years, as we know from the tombs of the pharaohs. By 1500 B.C., Egyptian glassmakers had perfected their art to include sacred ointment jars and vases, which were more precious than gold and jewels. Caesar and Cleopatra toasted their love in wine poured from decorated glass vessels into gorgeous glass goblets.

Until the Crusades the secrets of glassmaking remained in Alexandria and Byzantium, and feudal kings and nobles paid kings' ransoms for glassware from the East. Part of the booty the Crusaders brought back to Europe was Eastern glassware, but they brought back an even more important treasure: captured glassmakers with their secrets.

European glassmaking began to flourish during the Middle Ages, particularly in Venice. The stained glass windows of the great Gothic cathedrals, like Notre Dame, were their pride and glory. Even today they retain their awe-inspiring beauty. So precious were the products of the glassmakers' art that Venice prescribed a list of Draconian penalties for any glassmaker who divulged the Venetian processes abroad. The mildest penalty was tearing out the culprit's tongue.

The art of glassmaking gradually spread through Europe and came to America in the seventeenth century. Simple, early American bottles are very valuable today, some of the rarest having been sold to collectors and museums for thousands of dollars.

Because of the advances of modern technology, today's automated glass industry spews forth millions of bottles in America alone. They come in a thousand shapes and in hundreds of colors. Surely Cleopatra would have exchanged a Nubian slave bearing pearls for any one of these modern bottles with their beautiful colors and their delightful shapes. These bottles are your raw material—and most of them are free.

As soon as you've mastered the simple fundamentals of bottle art and spent a few dollars for equipment, you can begin to make useful and decorative items out of old bottles. With a little more practice, you can turn trash into treasures—you'll be a bottle artist. Your biggest bonus will not be the money you may get from selling your creations, nor even the admiration of your family and friends. It will be the tremendous satisfaction you feel in discovering within yourself a creativity you may never even have suspected.

Bottle art is simply the technique of cutting bottles neatly and precisely at predetermined points to make a host of beautiful items out of the cut segments. For example, cut off the bottom section of a wine bottle, smooth the cut edge, and you have a magnificent tumbler, while the top section can be either a funnel or a bell or a candlestick or a wind chime. As a matter of fact, either section can become any one of innumerable useful and decorative objects. You're limited only by your imagination.

Combine the cut bottle sections with leather, metal, plastic metal, paint, string, raffia, or any one of an endless variety of craft materials.

You'll wind up with handsomely unique gadgets that include lamps, ashtrays, serving bowls, dip dishes, cups, canisters, vases, pots, and almost anything else you can imagine.

The tools are cheap. Three different bottle cutters are now available. All of them work, although you may find one variety easier to handle. It's an individual matter, and you'll find craftsmen who swear by each one of the different types. Whichever one you select, a total investment of less than twenty dollars will put you on the road to fun and inventiveness.

If the tools are cheap, the materials are almost free, and with a little scavenging, they're completely free. For the basic starting material, an empty bottle, rummage through the trash at home, investigate the contents of your neighbor's rubbish pile, or scout the area just before trash pickup time. Chances are good that you can latch onto enough types, sizes, and shapes of bottles to carry you through several weeks of delightful and creative activity.

A basic tenet of all art is, *Form follows function*. For this reason the basic product turned out from cut bottles is pleasingly artistic. Bottles are basically functional, and you're starting out with a basic and pleasing geometric shape, a cylinder.

There is no reason why you can't pursue the artistic aspects of the craft and evolve bottle art into a true art form. You don't necessarily have to wind up with an article that is useful. The sections of glass can be put together with clear epoxy glue to form sculpture or assemblages. Artists employ the same idea with wood, metal, and plastic. Why not with glass? You may be the Alexander Calder or Jackson Pollack of a new art form.

Bottle art doesn't require a great amount of space. It's an ideal kitchen-table activity. Cleaning up is fast and easy. You can stop work at any point and tuck the project away until you are ready to resume activity. Unlike such hobbies as woodworking, there's no noise at all connected with bottle art. You can get involved in a particular project and work far into the night without getting angry telephone calls from your neighbors or heavy-lidded looks from your family the next morning.

Then, too, bottle art imposes no time urgency. You can work at it when you feel in the mood, put it aside when you've had enough, then pick it up again whenever you're ready.

Here's a golden opportunity to become personally involved in ecology. In a very pleasant way, you'll be recycling trash into beautiful and useful items. Think about that for a moment. Start out with the discarded raw materials that abound in every household, ranging from soft-drink bottles to vintage-champagne containers, not to mention maple-syrup jugs and those big gallon carboys that household bleach comes in. These days we get few opportunities to transform junk into something beautiful, but here's an excellent opportunity.

There's also a potential for making money in this craft activity. A few minutes of your time and some materials costing only pennies can result in a truly handsome item that you can sell for dollars. Markups of this extent spark wild enthusiasm on the part of any manufacturer. There's no reason why you can't transform bottles into dollars. Chapter VII details some straightforward moneymaking ideas.

This book contains all the information you need to know about this exciting new craft hobby and includes a gallery of projects that you can duplicate directly or use as jumping-off points for your own creative ideas. In either case, have fun!

II Where to Get Bottles

At first glance, this seems to be an unbeatable hobby from a cost standpoint. After all, the basic material is an empty bottle. Unhappily, as you develop expertise, you'll find it's increasingly difficult to locate enough empty bottles. Castoffs from your own household are limited. By the same token, your friends' and neighbors' castoffs are also limited. Any ordinary household in the process of day-to-day living can use only a limited number of bottles. Deep as their love for you may be, your friends and neighbors can't step up the availability of empties to any appreciable extent. The odds are that you'll tap the neighborhood resources in a relatively short time.

Restaurants, bars, clubs, and resorts have empties. However, federal law forbids the sale or reuse of liquor bottles and most bottle companies actually stamp that legend right into the bottles at the factory. (When you cut the bottle, of course, you no longer have a bottle and are not breaking the law by using the parts.)

Check the liquor laws in your community because there are restrictions that commercial drinkery establishments must abide by. In most areas liquor bottles must be destroyed when they are empty. Some major hotels have an employee whose sole job is to smash empty liquor bottles and there are even machines made for this purpose. They can break the glass and compact it into a neater bundle. For this reason, the availability of liquor bottles may be limited.

Wine bottles do not face the same restrictions. Wine bottles can be reused legally, so most restaurants, bars, and clubs are delighted to give them away as long as this doesn't create any additional problems for them. To get best results supply the eatery with sturdy cartons and give the porter a dollar or two. Instruct him to segregate empty wine bottles and pack them into the cartons you provide. Then, on a regular schedule, stop by with new cartons and lug off the full ones.

Scavenging is not as neat a way of acquiring the raw material, but in many instances it is quite effective. Check your local sanitation regulations. Restaurants and bars in some communities can put out their garbage when they close. In other communities they are more rigidly regulated and can only put out the garbage an hour or so before it is due to be picked up.

A little investigation will determine whether community regulations regarding the separation of garbage and trash are being observed. Theoretically, empty bottles are considered trash and should not be mingled with the potato peelings. This of course is an observation that you'll have to make on a first-hand basis.

In more rural areas you'll be able to avail yourself of the town dump. Such a facility offers the bonus of additional revenue. In a dump that has been in use for a long time, you'll sometimes find rare or unusual bottles. These are worth much more intact, since the value of a rare bottle is greatly diminished once it is segmented. Be alert and check such a bottle before you start cutting.

If funds aren't a problem, get in touch with a local trash-collection outfit. In exchange for some cash (the exact amount will vary according to demand and haggling ability), many of these outfits will put aside the specific type of bottle you want. Considering that they normally get only a penny or so for a bottle, be a sport and bid as high as a nickel or a dime. Money talks.

To find trash dealers that handle only used bottles, check the classified telephone directory. The big advantage here is sanitation. Most of these dealers have bottlewashing equipment, and for a small additional payment, they generally wash and sterilize the bottles besides selling you any quantity you specify.

The current emphasis on ecology and pollution control has created a bonus for the bottle cutter. Many communities now have recycling depots, where all sorts of trash is segregated and collected for reuse. Most of them don't really care how the material is reused, as long as it isn't recycled into instant trash. Depending upon the situation, you, as a public-spirited citizen, can show up with a station wagon and cart away interesting bottles. Your welcome will naturally be even warmer if you make a small donation to further the work of the recycling depot.

There's another possibility. Let's say your hobby has grown enormously. Demand is skyrocketing, and you have friends, relatives, neighbors, and strangers plucked off street corners working under your direction. Dealers all over the country are clamoring for your products. In such a happy situation you'll quickly outstrip most of the sources already covered, and you'll have to seek out new-bottle dealers in the classified telephone directory. In this case, you can specify the exact type, color, shape, and size bottles that you want, purchasing them in carload lots if you wish.

One advantage slightly offsets the added expense of buying from a new- or used-bottle dealer. You won't have to peel or soak off the labels; there are none.

III Types of Cutters and How to Use Them

Although there are several different types of cutters on the market, and although they work in slightly different ways, the process of cutting a glass bottle is basically the same two-step affair.

First, score a ring around the outside of the glass bottle at the point where you want it to break.

Second, create stress by tapping or by alternating heat and cold. The bottle will snap at the score mark.

In capsule, that's the routine. The score mark creates a weak area, then the hot and cold treatment creates a strain in the glass until it goes *ping!* at the precise point where you want it to come apart.

There's a very important element of luck here. Since glass bottles are not handcrafted objects but are turned out in enormous quantity by automated machinery, there are bound to be variations in the thickness of the glass. This happens most often with larger bottles, such as gallon jugs. Frequently, there will be thick and thin areas, and you'll never be able to tell in advance which one you're hitting. Depending upon your skill and patience, you should be able to get a proper cut at least seventy-five percent of the time. With a bit of practice, you'll soon achieve the desired result ninety-five percent of the time.

One general rule that applies to all cutting techniques is, *Don't force*. The score mark around the bottle is made with a glasscutting wheel. The trick here is, Use just enough pressure to score the glass. In this process, you are penalized for heavy-handed enthusiasm.

You can do the scoring by ear. When the cutter is aligned properly and there's just the right amount of pressure between the cutter and the glass, you'll hear a soft ripping sound as if someone were shredding old desk blotters. A crunching sound or a white, frosty-looking score mark means that you've been carried away by your own strength. As a result, the odds are stacked against your getting a clean, neat break in the glass. Remember, your goal is a thin, clean score mark.

Dirt on the bottles will dull the glasscutting wheels, so clean all bottles thoroughly before you start. Soak them in hot, soapy water for twenty or thirty minutes. Use a single-edge razor blade to scrape off the labels. (A double-edge blade should never be used since it cuts both ways, the second way being into your fingers.) Scrub the bottles to remove the last traces of glue. When they are well rinsed and dry, you're ready to start work.

Scraping off a label

Apply a drop of cutting oil to the turning wheel of the glasscutter each time that you use it. This will not only give you a better cutting action, but will also keep glass slivers from popping loose from the sides of the cut.

The hot-wire bottle cutter

Make sure that the cutting wheel is at a perfect right angle to the glass surface. Depending on the type cutter you use, there are all sorts of adjustments for this—some more complex than others.

HOT-WIRE CUTTER

Although slightly more expensive, a hot-wire cutter probably gives the most reliable results and is relatively foolproof. Sold by American Handicrafts Company, Fort Worth, Texas, it's available in their retail stores or by mail.

Scoring with a hot-wire cutter

The boxlike housing of the bottle cutter has a glasscutting wheel set into position at one end, side rails to cradle the bottle, and an adjustable sliding-block backstop. Place the bottle on the rails and move the sliding section forward until it rests against the bottom of the bottle. Hold it in place by tightening the wing nut.

Press down very lightly—just enough to hold the bottle in position against the glasscutting wheel—and rotate the bottle. Listen for that soft scoring noise. That's the tipoff of a proper cut. If at all possible, try to make the score mark in one even turn without stopping. It takes a little dexterity, but you'll get the hang of it after a while. The object is to wind up with a thin, clean, unbroken score mark all the way around the bottle.

Heating the score mark

The other end of the bottle cutter contains a heating element. Turn the bottle around and slide it along the rails until it's directly in line with the heating wire. Loop the wire around the bottle and carefully fit it into the score mark that you've made with the glasscutter.

Press down on the tension lever to tighten the wire around the bottle, then turn on the heating element. After a short while, you'll hear a little crackling sound. Keep the heat on until you can see a fracture line running almost all the way around the bottle. Quite likely, the little section at the bottom, where the glass isn't in contact with the wire, will not fracture.

Ease up on the tension lever a bit, release the heating-element button, and turn the bottle a half rotation on the rails. Fit the wire into place again, tighten down on the tension lever, and turn on the current once more. This time, the unfractured segment will be at the top, where it gets full heat from the wire. Keep the current on until this last section crackles, and you should have a fracture line all the way around the bottle.

Tapping the fracture line

The bottle may snap apart without any further help from you, but if it doesn't, and if the fracture line is complete, just tap it very lightly with the handle of a plastic or wooden tool. One or two gentle taps should be enough to separate the two segments.

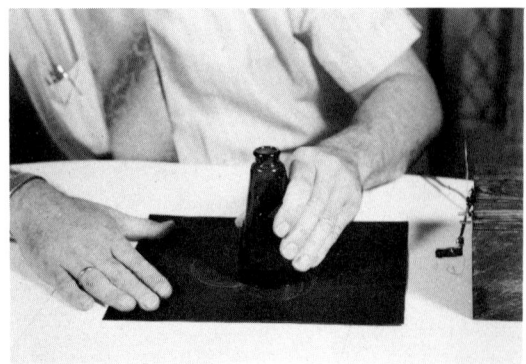

Smoothing the cut

Use emery paper to smooth the newly cut edges. Be very careful if you hold the emery paper in your fingers while you try to smooth the edges of the glass. It will take more time, but it will be safer if you place the sheet of emery paper flat on the surface of the table and rotate the bottle back and forth on top of it. Stop every now and then to check the edge. Properly smooth, it should be frosty in color all the way around. Shiny edges are a warning that more grinding is needed.

TAP CUTTER

Also quite popular is the tap-type bottle cutter, which uses a metal jig to hold the glasscutter in position on the outside of the bottle. (This gadget has several different adjustments to properly align cutter and bottle.)

Scoring a bottle

Holding the cutter in position, rotate the bottle. Once again, use only the amount of pressure that will produce a continuous, tiny, scratching sound. A deep, grinding cut that produces a frosty-looking score mark is almost guaranteed to give trouble when you try to separate the two sections.

Using the tapping rod

Insert the proper-sized tapping rod into the bottle, then very gently, with the tapper swinging away from you, clink it against the inside of the bottle exactly opposite the score mark. Tap very gently at first, then increase the force very slightly until a fracture occurs, perhaps one-half inch wide right along the score line. Move the tapper along the score mark until it is just about one-eighth of an inch ahead of this fracture mark, then tap again. Keep up this routine, tapping until the glass fractures, then shifting the contact point until it is about one-eighth inch ahead of the new fracture line. When you have a clean fracture line all the way around the bottle, the two halves will come apart.

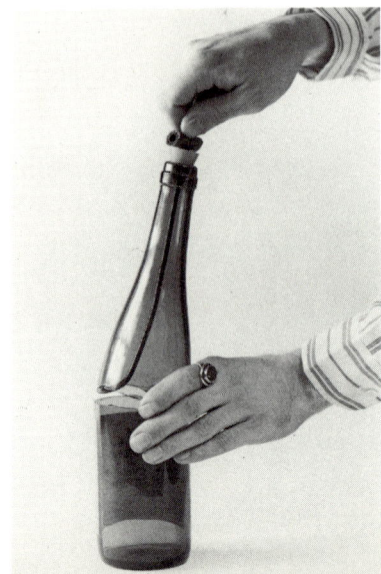

A clean break

FLAME-TYPE CUTTER

Like the hot-wire cutter, the flame-type cutter cradles the bottle so that it is at a right angle to the cutting wheel.

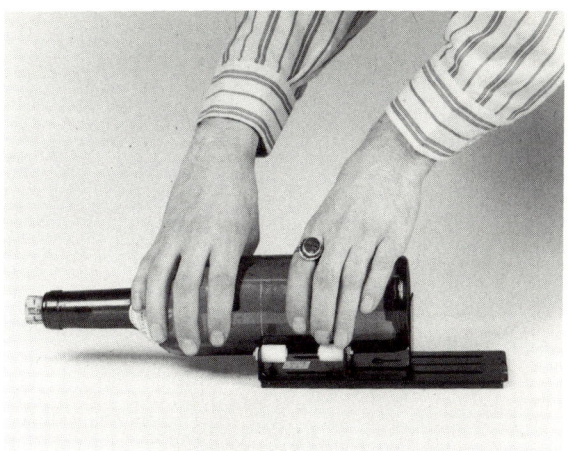

Cradle-type cutter

To score a mark all the way around the glass, hold the bottle firmly in place as you rotate it in the cutter, then rotate the score mark in a

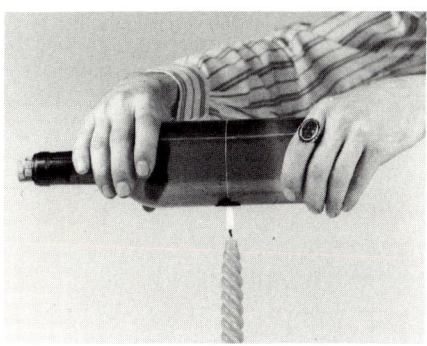

Heating the cut

candleflame. Make one or two turns with the flame directly on the score line, then a couple of more turns with the glass held a little further away from the flame to disperse the heat over a slightly wider area.

Cooling the cut

Rub the score line with an ice cube. The combination of the heat from the flame and the cold from the ice cube causes a stress in the glass that will start a fracture line. If the bottle sections do not separate, repeat the process with more heat and then with more cold. In stubborn cases you may have to go back and forth several times.

Don't, under any circumstances, try to score the same spot twice. If you go over the same area twice, you'll not only make the cut almost impossible to separate, but you'll also probably ruin the cutting wheel too. Remember, the objective is a clean, continuous, very thin line. On the other hand, if you miss a spot, you can, very carefully, go back over that tiny area.

It's a little difficult to describe a fracture line, although you'll immediately recognize it once you see it. It's simply the tiny score mark that you make on the outside of the bottle being extended all the way through the thickness of the glass until there's a tiny crack connecting inside and out. At first, the crack won't run all the way around the bottle, so keep tapping, or heating, until you have a continuous fracture line.

Like the mercury in a thermometer, a fracture line is visible only if it's viewed from the proper angle. Head on and at eye level, you probably won't be able to spot it. Try viewing it from a position slightly above the fracture line—just shift around a little until you can see it clearly. Viewing light also makes a difference. The fracture line will be more visible when you have the glass between you and the light. Here again, a little experimentation gets the technique down pat.

It's very important that you wear protective goggles during all phases of the cutting operation. Although the chances of a piece of glass popping loose and flying out at you are almost nonexistent, just the same, no matter how remote, the possibility *is* there. So why take chances when it's so easy to be safe. Bottle art is not by any stretch of the imagination a dangerous or hazardous task, but as in any craft where you use tools, the old maxim still applies—it's better to be safe than sorry.

OLD-FASHIONED METHOD

To get some idea of how lucky you are to have available today's foolproof, simple, and inexpensive equipment, take a look at the system used in your father's day. It may help to explain why bottle cutting didn't catch on until very recently as the satisfying and delightful hobby it is.

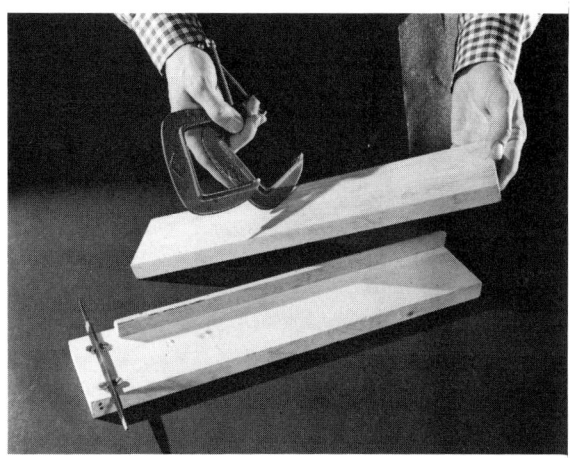

A hand-built jig

To start the process, you had to build the jig. The bottle rested on the wooden rails, and the backstop kept it in position. Instead of a glasscutter, most craftsmen used a new three-cornered file.

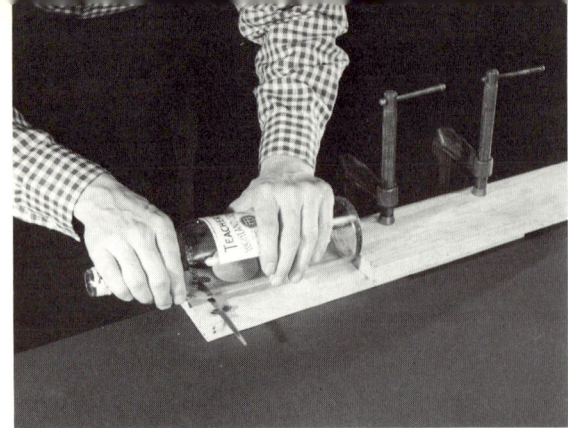

A handmade cutter

As in the modern process, you had to rotate the bottle against the file to make a score line all the way around the glass.

Tying the cord

Soaking the cord

Lighting the cord

Cooling the bottle

To create heat, a length of butcher's twine was tied around the bottle right at the score mark. It was saturated with benzene and set afire. Just when the flame died out, you plunged the bottle, neck down, into a bucket of cold water.

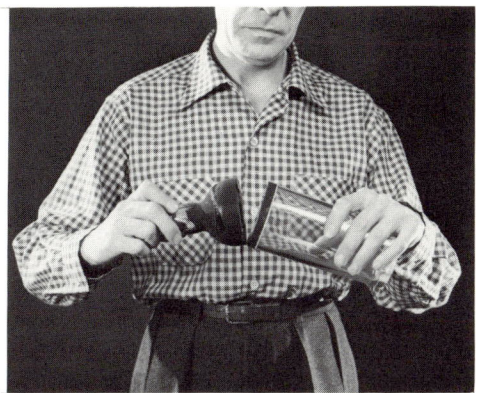

A lucky break

Luck was a much bigger element in those hazardous days. If you were very lucky, the two sections of the bottle separated easily and cleanly, but the success rate was rarely better than one in five.

Hand-finishing the cut

In addition the cut edges weren't as clean as those produced by today's bottle cutters, and you had to knock off the worst of the irregularities with a carborundum stone soaked in water before you could start grinding with emery paper.

SMOOTHING EDGES

Follow a regular routine to smooth the cut edge of a bottle. If you're going to do the job by hand, place a sheet of #60 emery cloth grit side up on a flat surface. Position the cut edge of the glass on the emery and rotate it back and forth against the grit. The wrist action does the trick. Shift over to a fresh section of the emery cloth whenever it shows signs of wearing smooth.

Smoothing the cut

When the edge of the glass is evenly frosted all the way around, it's time to shift to a #80 grade of emery cloth. Follow the same routine for a few minutes, then hold the glass at an angle while you lightly rotate it against the abrasive. The idea here is to gently round off both the inside and the outside edges so that the rim will be slightly rounded.

For a first-class job, finish off with a #220 emery cloth. This is generally sold in a variety known as wet-or-dry and means just that. You get better results by sprinkling a little water on the emery before you start to grind. Work away until the edge is smooth enough to suit you.

Be very careful not to rub the sides of the glass against the emery—the glass will wind up with unsightly scratches that are almost impossible to remove.

If you prefer to power up for this phase of the job, you can fit a disk sander to the chuck of your electric drill. The work will go a great deal faster, and because it requires less energy, you'll probably wind up with a much better edge. Use the same progression of abrasives here, starting with #60 grit, then using #80, and finally sanding with #220 wet-or-dry.

If you can get a bench stand for your electric drill, plus a little supporting table to rest the glass on, the job will be easier. It's almost impossible to align the glass and the sanding disk when both are handheld.

If you're really kneedeep in power tools, don't neglect a standard disk sander for this job. It's already fastened down to a bench or stand, and it has a supporting table in the proper position.

Wear protective goggles when you power-sand glass. The fine dust swirling off the abrasive wheel can cause extensive damage to your eyes. Don't run this risk when prevention is so easy.

There are other techniques for smoothing a cut edge. For example, some bottle-cutter kits come with a small supply of emery powder. Mix this with water and put it on a sheet of glass or on a flat, metal surface. The rest of the routine is the same. Smooth the cut edge by rotating it back and forth on the surface coated with emery paste.

Some craftsmen like to use the emery cloth discarded by floor sanders. The rough particles have already been knocked off the emery, and it's perfectly usable for smoothing glass.

Other types of abrasives will also do the job if you care to experiment a bit. Some grinding wheels work quite well, although you'll need several, ranging from coarse to fine.

No matter what type of abrasive you use, the procedure is pretty much the same. Coarse abrasives grind down the glass to give a flat surface and a slightly rounded edge. Finer abrasives, like #220 wet-or-dry emery cloth, remove the white, frosted appearance and actually polish the edge.

If you do any extensive power-sanding, wear a painter's mask or respirator. Available at almost any paint or hardware store, they're comfortable and inexpensive. As any woodworking hobbyist who works with power sanders can tell you, they're worth their weight in gold—the filter strains out the fine dust so that it can't reach your lungs.

Fire polishing is the only technique that gives an absolutely smooth edge to a glass object. Decidedly on the tricky side, the process takes time, requires skill, and carries no guarantee of success. If you're not entirely discouraged by these qualifications, here's how to do it.

Using standard abrasive technique, smooth the edge of the glass. Place the glasses in the kitchen oven while it is cool. Slowly raise it to as hot a temperature as it will go. When the glasses are hot, take them out one at a time and rest them on a wood or asbestos surface, so that there will be no drastic change in temperature.

With a blowtorch or a bottled-gas torch, heat the rim of the glass until it glows red and the glass actually melts slightly. To avoid creating too much stress in the glass, try to heat the entire circumference to about the same temperature at the same time. When you've finished a glass, put it back in the oven and start work on the next one.

As soon as you've completed the entire batch, temper the glass by lowering the oven temperature fifty degrees every half hour. When the temperature is down to about 150 degrees, shut off the heat. Keep the oven door closed and allow the heat to gradually drop until it reaches room temperature. This routine eases internal stresses set up in the glass by heating and melting the rim.

SPECIAL CUTTING TECHNIQUES

After you've become sufficiently immersed in this hobby, you may begin to champ at the limitations imposed by the cutting jigs. For one thing, almost all the jigs are designed for straight cuts; angle cuts are a little beyond their range. However, if you're willing to spend a little more time, you can open up whole new horizons with handcutting. One example of this technique is the plant container shown in Project 31. The oval-shaped hole in the side of the bottle was made with a hand-held cutter.

Using either masking tape or a felt marking pen, mark off the position of the cut. Very carefully, holding an ordinary glasscutter in your hand and following the guide markings, score the glass. All the same rules apply: use light, even pressure to produce a thin, fine line, and go over the surface only once. Then, working with a tapper inside the bottle, start a fracture line along the score mark. You'll probably have better results if you tap just slightly toward the center of the oval you've scored rather than right on the score mark. Work carefully and gently. If all goes well, there will be a slight pop, and a neat, oval piece of glass will detach itself from the side of the bottle.

If this technique doesn't work on the first try, or for that matter on the tenth, don't be too disappointed. Eventually you'll get the hang of it and have one more creative effect available for your use.

DRILLING HOLES IN GLASS

There may be times when you want to drill a small round hole in a glass bottle. If this is the type of project that you aren't likely to tackle too often, your best bet is to have the job done by a professional glasscutting shop. If you insist on keeping the entire project a cottage industry, use a really sharp, carbide-tipped twist drill mounted in a drill press. Rest the bottle on a sandbag placed on the platform of the press. Adjust the drill press to the slowest possible turning speed. Make a dam of putty around the spot you want to drill so that you can fill the center of the putty dam with water. Drill slowly and evenly, lifting the drill bit at frequent intervals to keep the heat from building up.

IV Safety Precautions

As far as danger is concerned, the *do*s and *don't*s of cutting bottles make up a relatively small list. Basically it's not a dangerous hobby. After all, glass certainly doesn't explode, nor does it jump up at you. If you insist upon being injured during the course of this hobby activity, you'll have to do something outrageously stupid; the normal exercise of very ordinary caution will keep you safe and sound. When glass breaks, the cut edges are going to be sharp. Recognize and remember this fact.

As a practical matter, there are really only a few rules for handling glass in this hobby. First of all, move slowly.

Have you ever watched men installing huge plate-glass windows in stores? Most of the time they look like they're loafing on the job. They're not. They're using their heads. When they're going to move a jumbo hunk of glass, they check the spot where it's resting, decide where and how they're going to hold it, then they check the spot where they're going to move the sheet. Very carefully, very slowly, they lift up the glass. Without any rush, and with great deliberation, they carefully move it to the new location and put it down very gently.

It's been said that many years ago, before there were such things as unions, whenever a glass-installation man broke one of those large sheets of glass, he had to pay for it. True or not, the fact remains—these men move with forethought and skill.

Be wise and take a tip from these professionals.

There's absolutely no reason to hustle and bustle about—certainly not when you can be damaged by your own haste. Before you act, take a few seconds to think about what you're going to do. Decide how you're going to accomplish it. Then, gently, slowly, and surely, do the job.

Just use ordinary garden-variety common sense. You don't have to be an intellectual giant. For example, some of the bottle-cutting techniques described in this book utilize heat to separate the sections of glass, and there's no need to be burned. Just keep your fingers away from the hot cutting wire or heated surfaces of the glass.

Don't work when you're tired. If you do, you'll make mistakes and do dumb things. Besides, what's the fun of a hobby if you have to pursue it to exhaustion? Tackle the craft at a time when you're rested and interested in having a good time. Why take the fun out of it?

Never force a tool; allow the tool to do the work. Maybe a little more time or patience is required. Maybe the tool is dull and you should sharpen or replace it before going on. Whatever the reason, find out the cause and correct it before you proceed. By the same token, keep tools in good working condition. If there are cutting edges that can rust, make sure that all moisture is removed and that the cutting edges are coated with a thin film of oil between jobs. Then, when you want to start work again, they'll be ready to use.

Be especially careful to protect your eyes. When actually snapping bottles in two, and especially when grinding the edges, be sure to wear protective goggles and gloves. Finding a doctor to remove a sliver of glass from your eye creates a discouraging atmosphere for any further hobby work. And yet, because this type of accident is so easily prevented, it falls into the category of a dumb mistake—one that you can easily avoid.

Make sure your work surface is clean at all times. The best procedure is to use a small vacuum cleaner. There's something definitely disquieting about pressing your elbow down firmly onto a glass sliver.

To compact glass remnants, wrap them carefully in several layers of old newspapers, dump them into a canvas sack, and clout the outside surface with a mallet. Finally, dump the remains into a sturdy, well-labeled carton.

As you work, sort out the pieces of cut glass that you plan to use for future projects. Whenever possible, store them on sturdy shelves—don't just jumble them together in a box. Not only will you be able to keep tabs on your stock of such segments, but they'll also remain in condition for future use. Rattling around like a bucket of bolts, the edges will become chipped and you'll become a sure candidate for an abrasion—just from rummaging through your box of goodies.

In the same manner, get rid of the broken pieces that you can't use; don't allow them to accumulate. Pack them into sturdy, well-marked, small-size cartons and seal the cartons carefully before adding them to the rubbish pile. Get a bright red large-tip felt marker so that you can identify the outside of the cartons with the words *Danger—Broken Glass*. Every rubbish collector will regard this as a humane gesture.

One final word. Keep in mind that certain processes involved in this craft activity may lead to future hazards if instructions aren't followed properly. As an example, there may be instances where you want to get a smooth-fired edge around the rim of a newly cut and ground tumbler. As described in the how-to section of this book, this is done with heat. However, unless you follow the procedure all the way through and place the glass in an oven, where the temperature is slowly raised and then slowly lowered, you're going to create uneven stress within the glass. This means that a week later, or a month later, the glass can be just sitting quietly on the shelf when suddenly there'll be a *ping!* and the glass will shatter into pieces. What happened is that the stresses in the glass built up to the point where tension overpowered the glass itself. This *ping!* may be slightly embarrassing while the tumbler is sitting quietly on the shelf, but you'll suffer a great deal more chagrin if this tiny explosion occurs just as you're reaching for the glass to pour your boss a drink at a cocktail party.

V Types of Glass

No matter what anybody tells you, all glass is not the same. Not only can the glass be made from different combinations of materials, but it can also be either thick or thin—and unhappily, there can be variations of thickness in the same bottle.

Smooth-sided soda bottles as well as most of the beer bottles around these days fall into two general categories: returnables and nonreturnables. Returnable bottles have to be thicker than those designed for one-time use; thus they require more glass. Nonreturnable bottles are therefore easier to cut.

Stay away from Coca-Cola bottles—at least in the beginning. Not only is the glass thick but it's also highly irregular due to the pattern that's embossed in the sides. As a result, these bottles are difficult to cut.

Also forget about square or odd-shaped bottles until you develop expertise. These bottles have to be scored by hand or with some sort of homemade jig. It's at best a very uncertain process and there's just no sense adding this kind of complication to the work.

Uneven thickness in the walls of a glass bottle often occurs in larger-size bottles such as gallon jugs. Frequently you won't spot the problem until you start tapping to separate the two sections. Then you'll come to one spot with a perfectly adequate score mark that still refuses to fracture. When this happens, reverse course and start tapping in the other direction—at the other end of the fracture line. Eventually, you'll be back at the problem spot. However, this time, because there's a fraction line at both sides of the thick spot, there's a better chance that the bottle will separate along the score mark.

Don't practice on valuable antique-glass bottles or vases. For the most part this is a task best left to professionals. As a matter of fact, if you merely confine your early practice sessions to evenly contoured nonreturnable beer bottles, you'll quickly build up that feeling of unshakable confidence that every successful craftsman enjoys.

Keep in mind that there's a certain degree of chance and caprice that operates in the bottle-cutting craft. For instance, you can snap five ginger-ale bottles in a row without a single bit of trouble, then the sixth one skews off at an angle instead of following the score mark. Why? No special reason. Just accept the odds. Next time your luck will be better.

Just as credit-card companies maintain a deadbeat file, you'll gradually accumulate your own tally sheet of particular bottles that are difficult or impossible to cut. Coca-Cola bottles head the list, but they're by no means unique. If you want to avoid an undue amount of frustration, steer clear of these problem bottles.

VI Other Materials —Other Techniques

As you flip through the gallery of bottle-cutting ideas shown in this book, you'll realize that many of the effects require more than just cutting bottles. For example, sections of glass fastened together and combined with various types of decorative trim help make some of the beautiful and unusual objects shown. None of this is difficult, so here's a quick run-through of the techniques and materials you may want to use.

EPOXY GLUE

Use epoxy glue that dries in five minutes and is clear rather than silver or white in color. Most likely, it will come in two tubes, one containing hardener, the other resin (these two components of epoxy glue have to be kept separate).

Use a small piece of aluminum foil as a mixing surface, and squeeze out equal quantities of resin and hardener just before you're ready to use the glue. Use as much as you need—just be sure that the quantity squeezed out of each tube is the same. Mix the two sections together with a small stick. Be especially thorough; the glue will not set properly unless it has been completely mixed.

Make sure the surfaces to be joined are clean and free of grease. Apply the epoxy glue and brace the two sections in place for five minutes or so, until the glue has set. If you have to build up more epoxy glue, do it slowly and in thin layers rather than in one enormous glob that's guaranteed to ooze down where it's not wanted. When you're through with the job, carefully fold up the alumnium foil with the excess glue inside. It's wonderful stuff, but very difficult to get rid of on hands or furniture.

SILICONE ADHESIVE

Use clear silicone adhesive for most jobs (it also comes in white and gray). It's a superb adhesive for fastening glass to glass or for fastening almost any other material to glass. Although it doesn't set as quickly as the five-minute epoxy adhesive, it reaches a tacky stage in a relatively short time. Allow overnight drying to build up full strength.

DOUBLE-SIDED PRESSURE-SENSITIVE TAPE

The standard cellophane tape that's coated with a sticky adhesive on one side also comes with adhesive on both sides. Although the bond doesn't withstand hot water, alcohol, or most other potables, it is good for affixing trim to glass when the object is going to get light use. Available in most stationery stores, double-sided cellophane tape comes in several different widths.

PAPER TRIM

Paper trim is available from large stationery stores, art-supply stores, or, in major cities, from specialty paper-novelty supply stores. The gold and silver trim used on some of the items illustrated in the gallery section of this book are made of paper. In addition to finding borders and edgings, you'll probably also find a fairly extensive assortment of stars, angels, animal figures, and lots of charming, old-fashioned designs.

LACE TRIM

The notions counter of a large department or dime store is a good place to shop for this material because it is real lace. Of course, it's machinemade, but it adds a nice decorative touch at a very limited cost. Use silicone adhesive to hold both gold and lace trim to the glass.

PLASTIC METAL

Sold under various trade names, this material is actually fine aluminum or steel powder that's been mixed with glue of some sort. The end result is a shiny substance that you squish out of a tube; it dries to form a tough, hard material that's quite similar to metal in many respects. The handles on the measuring cups shown in the gallery section of this book are made out of plastic metal. In this particular case, the material was dabbed on in globs and left rough to simulate crude, medieval workmanship. If you prefer a smooth, shiny finish, just build up the material into a thicker layer, then file, sand, and buff it until it shines.

LEATHER

Thin, stiff leather seems to work out best for most purposes. Cut it to size, punch all necessary holes, then stain it to the color you want, using the dye meant for this purpose (it can be purchased from a craft-supply store). Allow the stain to dry thoroughly, then apply one or two coats of leather finish to protect the surface. Hold the leather to the glass with thong lacing or with silicone adhesive. If you're using glue, temporarily apply tape to hold the leather in position until the adhesive sets.

GLASS PAINT

Since most ordinary paints don't stick to glass, use the special paints that are specifically designed for this purpose. You can buy them in a

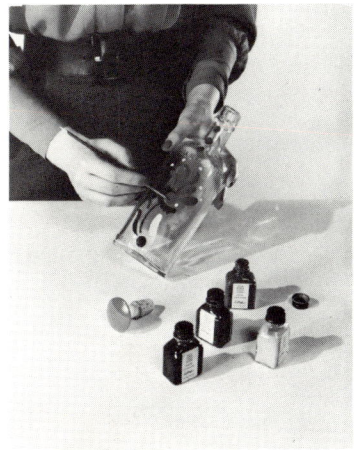

Painting a bottle

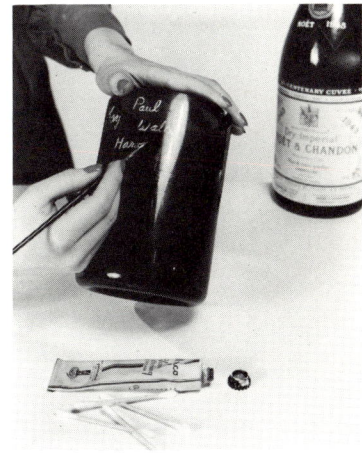

Lettering a bottle

rainbow-hued assortment at most craft-supply stores. Although they come ready-mixed in jars or tubes, they tend to be slow-drying, so don't plan on using these paints for any rush project.

TWINE

Colored twine or tightly woven yarn makes an excellent decorative accent for many bottle projects, but just wrapped around a bottle, it's

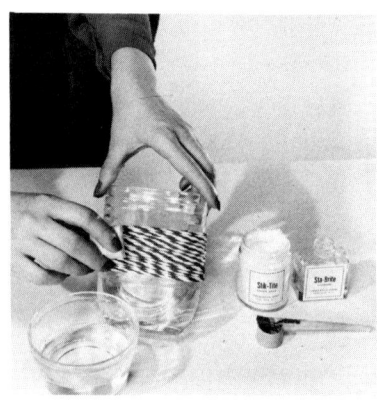

Applying colored string

sure to loosen in short order. Hold the string in place with an adhesive that dries colorless (it's a special item sold in craft-supply stores—or else use any white glue like Elmer's, diluted half and half with water). Coat the bottle with the glue, then wind the twine in place. Add another layer of glue on top, applying it with a sponge to hold the string in a neat wrapping and to protect the surface. When you're finished, sponge off any extra glue from the glass. If you prefer, you can also use clear plastic spray for the top surfacing.

Accenting with raffia

Raffia comes in long, loose hanks and is available in bright colors. Coat the bottles with white glue, then drape the raffia around the bottles. To keep the windings neat, dab the layers with a sponge soaked in a 50-50 solution of white glue and water. To add a protective coating to the decor, give the final layers a light sponging with the diluted glue. For a ropelike effect, twist the strands of raffia tightly together before wrapping them around the bottles. As before, use diluted white glue to hold the strands firmly in position.

Many of the materials described in this chapter are available in dime stores or department stores. Try large stationery or art-supply stores too. Perhaps the best all-around source is a craft-supply store. The largest outfit of this type, American Handicrafts Company, has several hundred retail stores scattered about the country. In addition, this company has an extensive mail-order operation with a well-illustrated, free catalog describing their bottle cutter plus all the decorative accessories used with bottle projects. If you can't buy materials locally, write them directly for a catalog; their address is PO Box 791, Fort Worth, Texas.

VII How to Make Money from Your Hobby

If you would like to cash in on your newfound craft interest, you're in luck—at least to a certain extent. Although bottle cutting has been around for some time, it's only now taking on the proportions of a national mania. Therefore, as far as the specific craft area goes, you're just slightly in advance of a solid wave of interest.

Although the tools and kits for bottle cutting are widely available, at this writing there isn't much in the way of finished craft objects being offered for sale through retail stores. Don't expect to find a fantastic, successful, get-rich-quick scheme outlined here. It's just not in the cards. Let's take an example. John M. Management is an executive who has taken up bottle cutting as a leisure-time activity. His wife admires his handiwork, his friends have asked for samples (free of course), and he's even interested a couple of local shops to whom he's proudly shown an assortment of tumblers, beer steins, and vases. The upshot of all this: he thinks to himself, Well, maybe there's a bit of money to be made here. And like any good executive, John sits down to work the numbers.

Right away there's a cost problem. You see, John has worked his way up pretty high in the corporate payscale. His yearly income, when figured out on the basis of a standard forty-hour week, works out to maybe ten to fifteen dollars an hour. John keeps tabs on his working time and he knows that to turn out a set of eight matched glasses with properly smooth edges takes a couple of hours. So what's the price that John should get for these glasses? Twenty dollars for the set? Thirty dollars for the set? No way! He'd be pricing himself so far above what the average customer would pay that all he'd wind up with for his effort would be a set of very expensive and unsold glasses.

Shift your thinking into another gear. Simply realize that although you can most likely make some extra money by doing the craft work you have found to be such fun, as a general rule you're not likely to get filthy rich at it.

It's possible to make a handsome profit through the manufacture and sale of bottle objects, but to make a living from your enjoyable hobby entails taking it out of the hobby category, working toward making it a fulltime business occupation, quitting the job you have now, and devoting as much time and effort to it as you have to your regular job or occupation. This is simply not realistic or practical for ninety-nine out of a hundred bottle artists.

You can, however, make some money out of your hobby as a part-time proposition on a modest scale. Here are some suggestions for setting up a small-scale craft business which will provide extra income from selling the things you make from cut bottles.

GET READY

Think about how much time and effort you wish to devote to your operation. Decide how many items you wish to sell and how much time each one takes. Figuring the value of your time, calculate the cost of producing a particular item and decide whether it makes economic sense in your particular case to produce that item; also decide whether it's worth your while to develop a complete line of ten to twenty different kinds of objects. The craft ideas in this book will give you a start.

The road to economic disaster is clearly marked by sloppy technique. Friends and relatives may regard uneven edges and other goofs as charming, but a customer who spends his hardearned money is far less tolerant. Concentrate on products that are relatively easy to make and seem to have the best sales potential. Use your friends as sales barometers. When they drop over, ask their opinions on which items they like best and how much they think the average customer would pay for them.

Take the items that make the most economic sense and visit your local gift and card shops. Ask the proprietors which items they think will sell and if they would be interested in carrying your products.

Having established the demand, carefully figure your costs on each item, including special trim or other materials, and approximately how much of your time each item will take. Decide how you're going to arrange your facilities and if you have sufficient working and storage space. Check the availability of needed materials and double-check prices as well as discounts for quantity purchases.

Guided by a realistic view of what the market will bear, establish a firm retail and wholesale price schedule for the various items. Finally, check local, state, and other business regulations—for example, you may need a sales-tax number. Set up a rudimentary bookkeeping system, keeping it as simple as possible—date and amount of sale; item sold; sales tax where indicated; and expenses for materials, labor, and any incidentals. Carefully recheck your costs and prices, and you're ready to go into business.

PROMOTION

A major problem is that so far only your family and friends know about you and the fantastically beautiful bottle-art objects that you have for sale. Advertising is vital in any business, but you can't afford full page ads in magazines—or even your local paper—without raising the prices of your work to astronomical levels. The solution is to get as much exposure and publicity as possible, with no cost in dollars and at the least possible cost in time and effort.

Your local chamber of commerce, various community groups, and sometimes local banks and stores, all sponsor exhibitions by local artists. That's you. If they want to quibble, you're a local craftsman, and an exhibition of your work will provide a beautiful display, particularly for a bank. Explain that you're perfectly willing to set the whole thing up for free and that all you want in return is to display your name, address, and telephone number as part of your bottle-art exhibit. Remember, what you're after is the exposure of your work to the maximum number of people.

Contact your local newspaper, shopping-center throwaways, and newsletters put out by churches and community groups. Show them what you're doing and there's a good chance that they'll run an item or even a feature story on your work.

Check on any craft fairs or flea markets in your area and find out what the charge is for setting up a small booth. These are ideal events for your handcrafted bottle art. At many of these outdoor fairs your sales counter is the tailgate of your station wagon.

Don't forget community bulletin boards and don't neglect the bulletin boards in supermarkets and shopping centers. If you have a circular or illustrated catalog sheet, ask if you can put it up. Use ingenuity instead of money to get the maximum publicity.

START SELLING

Go back to the stores that expressed interest in your products on your preliminary visits. This time offer each store a simple, attractive display of a few of the objects plus a simple, handlettered sign.

You'll probably have to sell on consignment, meaning that you'll have to leave your work with the store without receiving any money for it until it's sold. Get a receipt showing the exact merchandise the store received, the retail price for each item, and the retailer's discount, which will run in the neighborhood of forty to fifty percent. Call back on each sales outlet often enough to keep track of which items seem to be selling best and to replace the stock. If some items aren't moving at all, substitute different ones.

Display-advertising space in the larger newspapers is prohibitively expensive for a small-scale operation, but classified advertisements are considerably cheaper. A few words in a small amount of space can bring you many inquiries and many sales. Keep your advertisements simple—don't get flowery. Keep track of the ads you place and the response. Keep using the copy and the papers that bring you good response; drop those that don't.

If all else fails, or if you prefer this approach, set up your own shop, using the front porch, basement, or garage of your home. Check to make sure you're permitted to do so by local regulations, then put up a sign announcing that you're selling handcrafted bottle-art objects, and list the hours you'll be open for business.

Whether you spend an hour or two a day on your front porch and sell only a few items a week or wind up with a staff of a hundred artisans working in your bottle-art studio-factory and can no longer spare the time to make bottle-art items yourself, you'll have the added pleasure of making money out of a craft hobby that gives you pleasure and satisfaction.

Either way, good luck—and have fun.

A Gallery of Bottle-
Art Projects

VIII A Gallery of Bottle-Art Projects

Before beginning any of the projects that follow, bear certain things in mind. You'll be working with glass; unlike leather, wood, or even metal, glass doesn't bend or give—it breaks. When glass breaks, either by accident or along the score mark, which is really a break along a line you've already made in the surface of the glass, a break in glass always results in a cutting edge. *Never handle broken or newly cut glass with your bare hands.* When snapping bottles or when grinding the edges, *be sure to wear protective gloves.*

If you're using power tools to grind, smooth, or polish a glass edge, *never forget to wear protective goggles;* if it's going to take you more than a moment or two for the operation, *wear an inexpensive painter's mask* to protect your lungs from the fine particles of glass dust. You can always get another power tool, but you can't replace your hands, your eyes, or your lungs.

Working with glass isn't a dangerous craft, but use the same common sense that prevents you from crossing a busy street without looking to see if a car is coming. If you use your head and take sensible safety precautions, you'll never even get a scratch from a glass sliver. If you're careless and fail to take reasonable precautions, the results may be tragic.

The following projects aren't dangerous, difficult, or expensive. They're fun! Don't be in too much of a hurry, work slowly and carefully, and think of what you're doing as you take every step in a project.

Remember that bottle cutting is not only a craft but also an art. After you've gained a little experience and a sense of confidence, modify or vary the projects according to your taste and need. If you think a clear bottle would be better than the colored bottle suggested in the project instructions, use a clear bottle. Vary the sizes of the bottles slightly if you wish. Most of the following projects can be varied according to individual taste, although all of them are designed with an eye on practicality and appearance. You can use many of them as a starting point for your own ingenuity and imagination.

In the following projects, *every time you cut a bottle you must smooth and finish the cut before proceeding to the next step,* even if the instructions don't say so. Whenever epoxy is indicated, it's *clear* epoxy.

Many of the projects call for miniature liquor bottles of the airline type (these are the bottles individual drinks are sold in by the airlines). If you fly and have a drink, save the bottle; better still, before the end of your flight, ask the stewardess to let you have all the empties before you land; and finally, ask your friends to save theirs.

Some of the bottles designated in the projects (for example, Piels beer bottles) may not be available in your locality. If you're not familiar with the brand names in some of the projects, you can tell the type of bottle from the illustration and procure a similar bottle in your area. All the materials necessary for the projects are available anywhere in America. Look over the projects and choose the ones that appeal to you the most. It's not fattening—and it's fun!

HIGHBALL GLASSES

Project 1

Wine bottles are ideal for the purpose, but almost any thin glass bottles will do. Carefully soak off the labels before cutting, and iron them flat. Make the cut three and a half inches from the bottom of the bottles.

If you decide to glue the labels back on the finished glasses, you'll have a handsome set of unique highball glasses, each with a different label, making it easy for your guests to identify their own glasses when it comes to refills.

The last stage in construction is to carefully glue the thoroughly dry labels back on, using decoupage adhesive or silicone glue. When the labels are firmly set and the glue has dried, spray the label on the completed glass with clear plastic to form a protective coating.

ICED TEA GLASSES *Project 2*

Whisky-sour-mix bottles or any similar tall, slender bottles are appropriate for this simple project.

Most whisky-sour-mix bottles have a design just below the neck; cut the glass immediately below the design at the point where the straight section begins.

CANDLE CROWNS *Project 3*

This is another ideal project for whisky-sour-mix bottles or any other bottles with an interesting or pleasing design just below the neck. Cut the glass just below the design section.

The candle bells shown in the illustration are the top sections of the whisky-sour-mix bottles used in Project 2. If you cut carefully, you'll wind up with two projects from each bottle.

ICE CREAM SODA GLASS *Project 4*

Any glass bottle that is at least eight inches tall and about two and a half inches in diameter may be used for this project. Make the cut about six and a half inches from the bottom of the bottle, then measure a piece of thin, medium-stiff leather to fit snugly around the glass, allowing enough space for the lacing. Mark the positions of the lacing holes and punch out the holes with a leather hole-puncher.

You can stain the leather any color you wish to match your decor or suit your taste. After having stained and finished the leather, wrap it around the glass and lace it with a similar or contrasting leather thong. Knot the lacing at the bottom and tuck the ends under the leather. This handsome design is especially good for sodas or other cold liquids; the leather acts as an insulation to keep the contents cold.

CREAM PITCHER *Project 5*

Use a Log Cabin syrup bottle or any other interestingly shaped small bottle that has a pouring spout right above the handle.

For this project you must first score the glass right above the handle with a handheld glasscutter; then snap off the top portion using the candleflame–and–ice-cube method; and finally, carefully grind the glass with a small grinding stone to form the mouth of the pitcher.

For decoration carefully cut out the chosen design pictures and apply a coat of decoupage adhesive to the bottle where the pictures will be positioned; then brush another coat of the decoupage adhesive to the back of the design and press it down firmly onto the side of the pitcher. When the adhesive is thoroughly dry, coat the entire design area, including a thin rim of glass beyond it, with either decoupage varnish or clear plastic to protect the surface.

PILSNER GLASS *Project 6*

A Sangria bottle or any other bottle with a similar contour and a nice tapering shape to the neck can be used for this interesting project.

Make the cut at the point where the tapering neck ends and the straight sides of the glass begin. Also cut a round base from a matching colored bottle (most wine bottles will do nicely for the base).

Use clear epoxy to glue the mouth of the bottle to the center of the wine-bottle bottom which forms the base of the glass. Brace the two in position until the epoxy has set.

To produce glasses of different shapes, simply experiment with other combinations of bottles.

CHIP DISH *Project 7*

Almost any bottle can be used for this easy project. Clear-glass juice bottles are excellent and are easily obtainable.

Carefully soak off the label before the cut is made, then make the cut just above the label's former position. When the label is perfectly dry (if necessary, iron it until it's flat and dry), fasten the label to the completed project with decoupage adhesive or silicone glue.

This project also makes a fine container for jellies or other preserves that don't need to be kept tightly covered.

SUGAR BOWL *Project 8*

Use a Ripple wine bottle or any other bottle with an interesting design pressed into the glass. Make the cut about two or two and a half inches from the bottom of the bottle. You now have a sugar bowl which will enhance any breakfast table. An assortment of these make very nice condiment containers for the table.

FRUIT BOWL *Project 9*

Use a clear gallon jug and make the cut about seven inches from the bottom. You now have a simple and handsome fruit bowl which can also be used for a mixing bowl, a serving bowl, or even a goldfish bowl.

PRETZEL BOWL *Project 10*

Use any large, straight-sided bottle. A half-gallon Sangria bottle is excellent for this purpose. Make the cut just below the neck of the bottle at the point where the straight sides begin. This particular type of bottle is a little difficult to cut, so don't be discouraged by a higher than average failure rate.

The finished project also works out very nicely as an ice bucket or serving bowl for Sangria. *Olé!*

CANDY DISH *Project 11*

Use a quart beer bottle or almost any other bottle with similar dimensions. Make the cut about two inches from the bottom of the bottle. You can use the finished project for cocktail-hour dip dishes or for dessert bowls (they look particularly handsome in sets).

FRUIT BOWL *Project 12*

Use a gallon-size Almadén wine bottle and make the cut at the point where the bottle is widest in diameter. Because the glass in this type of bottle is very thin, it has a tendency to break irregularly, so work very carefully to avoid a higher than average failure rate.

For the base, cut a piece of three-quarter-inch wood into a six-inch square; then drill a hole in the center, which is found at the intersection of two light pencil lines drawn from the corners of the square (the lines are easily erased after you've marked your center point). To hold the mouth of the bottle snugly, drill a hole of the correct size almost all the way through the center of the wood; then sand the wood lightly, stain, and varnish the bottle to the wood base with epoxy glue. Presto! A very handsome fruit bowl.

CANDY DISH *Project 13*

Use an imported brandy bottle or any other bottle with thick glass sides and an interesting shape. Make the cut approximately one and a half inches below the point where the straight sides of the bottle begin.

For the base, make the cut three-quarters of an inch from the bottom of a contrasting or matching wine bottle. Attach the brandy-bottle top section to the base with epoxy glue and brace them in proper position until the adhesive has hardened. This project also makes an interesting champagne glass of classic shape.

MARTINI GLASS AND OLIVE HOLDER *Projects 14 and 15*

For the martini glass, use a Seven-Up bottle or any other clear glass bottle with an interesting design on the tapered section. Make the cut at the point where the straight sides of the bottle begin. The base of the martini glass is made from the top of a wine bottle, the cut being made four or five inches from the top. Fasten the two sections together with epoxy glue. A cork forced into the bottom of the top section and well coated with epoxy glue makes an effective waterproof seal.

The actual dimensions aren't so important as winding up with shapes pleasing to your particular eye. Depending on the bottles you're using and your individual taste, you may prefer to make the cuts at slightly different points.

The olive holder in the illustration was made from the bottom of a French champagne bottle, the cut being made about two and a half to three inches from the bottom.

The dimple that holds the olives is characteristic of champagne bottles made in France. Champagne is the only wine that ages in the bottle, and as the bubbly effervescence builds up, terrific pressure also builds up inside the bottle. This is the reason the cork has to be held in with a wire fastening.

The dimple blown in the bottom of the bottle is popularly supposed to strengthen the bottle against the danger of it exploding, which occasionally happens in the French caves where champagne is aged. When the second Baron de Rothschild was asked about this, he laughed uproariously, "Not at all. The bottles are made that way so that they look bigger and hold less champagne."

ASH TRAY *Project 16*

Use a brandy bottle for this project (the top section of a brandy bottle was used for the candy dish in Project 13), or use any other bottle that has a bell or dimple in the base, such as an imported champagne bottle. Make the cut about three inches from the bottom of the bottle.

PEACE-SIGN ASH TRAY *Project 17*

A half-gallon jug or any other large-diameter bottle is required for this project. Make the cut two inches from the bottom of the jug. With a pair of pliers, bend coat-hanger wire to form the crosspieces that support the cigarettes, then solder the wires together at the center and slip them onto the ash tray.

PENCIL HOLDER *Project 18*

A Seven-Up bottle or any other similar-size bottle with an interesting pattern on the side provides the raw material. Make the cut just at the point where the tapering neck of the bottle ends and the straight sides begin.

STRAW HOLDER *Project 19*

Use a Seven-Up bottle or any other similar-size bottle that has the label silk-screened on by the manufacturer. Make the cut approximately a half inch above the point where the *7-up* design ends.

This idea also provides handsome soda glasses for the younger set.

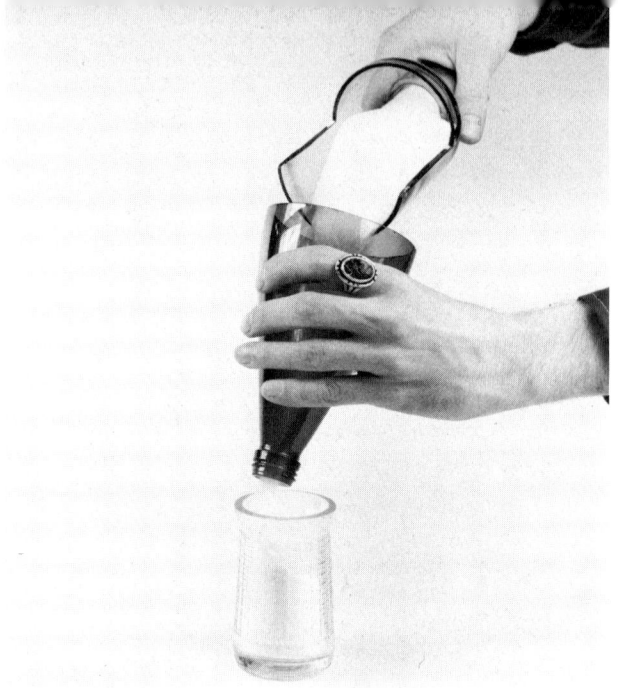

FUNNEL AND SCOOP *Projects 20 and 21*

For the funnel, use a nonreturnable beer bottle; for the scoop, use a wine bottle with a relatively straight neck rather than one with a tapered neck.

Make the cut for the funnel at the point where the curved section ends and the straight sides begin. The cuts for the scoop are more complicated. Make the first cut approximately three and a half inches from the bottom of the bottle, then score a line halfway around the bottle about four inches above the first cut. With a felt-tipped pen, mark guide lines for the perpendicular side cuts, then make the two side cuts with a handheld cutter. Tap *very carefully* to remove the half-section of glass.

Smooth the edges with a sanding disk or grindstone. Be sure to wear heavy gloves during the sanding and smoothing operation; the glass is relatively fragile and breaks easily. If you use a power-activated drill for the sanding disk, wear your goggles.

WALL PLANTER *Project 22*

A wine bottle or almost any bottle with the appropriate dimensions provides the material for this decorative wallpiece.

For your cut, consult the illustration and take into consideration the conformation of the bottle you've chosen. Mark the place where you want your cut to begin, using masking tape or a felt-tipped marking pen to make guide lines you can follow in making the oval cut; score the glass with a hand cutter; then tap carefully to separate the sections. Using silicone adhesive, fasten gold paper trim to the cut edge of the bottle and around the neck.

For the base, cut a piece of wood to size (about four by eight inches). Sand it smooth, then stain it and allow it to dry thoroughly. Fasten the bottle to the wood with epoxy glue.

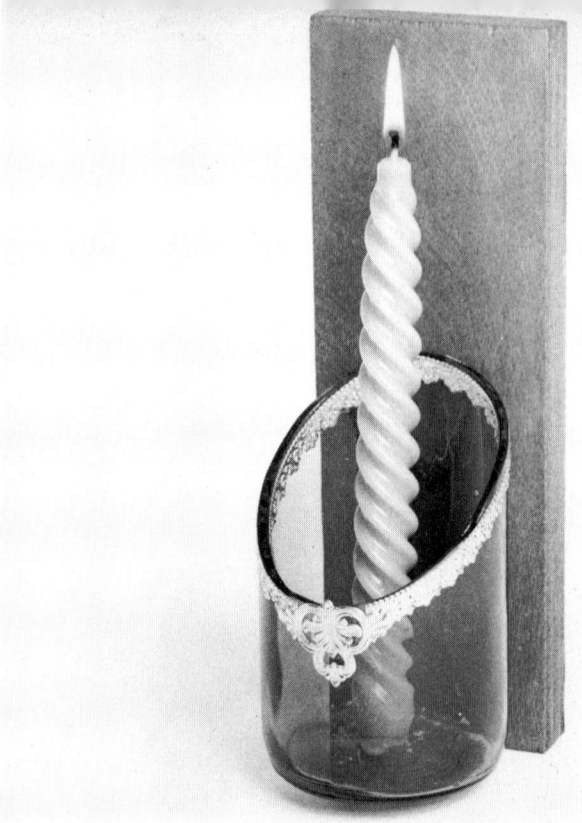

WALL CANDLE *Project 23*

Use a brown or green wine bottle or any other colored bottle that suits your decor or personal taste.

Mark off your guide lines for the oval cut with masking tape or a felt-tipped pen; use a handheld cutter to score the glass along the marked line; tap very carefully to separate the sections. Fasten gold paper trim to the cut edge with silicone adhesive; after the trim has dried thoroughly, coat it with clear plastic.

For the base, cut a piece of wood (approximately four by eight inches); sand it smooth; then stain it an appropriate shade or spray it with a clear plastic coating if you prefer the natural wood color of the piece you've chosen. When the wood has dried thoroughly, fasten the bottle to it with clear epoxy glue.

HANGING PLANTER Project 24

Use a straw-wrapped Chianti bottle or any other decorative bottle with a bulbous base. Make the cut just above the raffia wrappings. The planter is supported by braided leather thongs run through the edge of the raffia wrappings, or by coat-hanger wire similarly attached.

HANGING CLEAR-GLASS PLANTER   Project 25

For this planter, use a clear gallon jug. Make the cut three inches below the point where the tapered neck meets the straight sides. Fasten a cork in the mouth of the bottle with epoxy glue. The hanging supports are made of three leather thongs, each one a yard long. All three leather thongs are attached to a shorter length of leather wrapped around the bottle just below the finger grip and tied in place with a double knot.

LONG-STEMMED VASE

Project 26

Use a Guinness stout bottle or a similar bottle with an interesting taper and pleasant color for the vase section; make the cut approximately five inches from the top of the bottle. For the base, cut off the top portion of a Piels beer bottle. Fasten the two sections neck to neck with epoxy glue; force a cork down into the top portion of the vase; then thoroughly cover the cork with a layer of epoxy glue to form a waterproof seal.

STUBBY VASE   *Project 27*

Use a Seven-Up bottle or any other decorative glass bottle of a similar shape.

For this project make two cuts in the bottle, one just above the bumpy portion of the top and the other just above the bumpy portion of the bottom. Glue the cut segments of the top and bottom together, using epoxy adhesive. Make sure the junction is waterproof, applying additional epoxy if necessary.

In the illustration the neck has been cut off the bottle section forming the top of the vase; although it enhances the vase from a standpoint of design appeal, it's not absolutely necessary.

The decoration is a macramé design of colored string utilizing triple square knots alternating with a spiral of half-stitches decreasing to fit the diameter of the glass at the bottom. Feel free to substitute any pattern you prefer.

GOBLET-PLANTER   Project 28

Illustrated is a twelve-ounce Schmidt's nonreturnable bottle, but you can use any other colored-glass bottle of a similar shape and size.

Make the cut just below the point where the tapered neck meets the straight sides. Fasten the bottom section of the bottle on top of the mouth with epoxy glue. The illustration shows this project used as a small planter. It makes an equally attractive drinking goblet.

SMALL FLOWER VASE   *Project 29*

Use a long-necked wine bottle or any bottle of a similar shape to make this charming vase.

  There are two cuts to be made in this project: the first, half an inch below the point where the tapered neck meets the straight sides; the second, a half inch above the bottom of the bottle. After the cut edges have been sanded flat and smooth, fasten them together with epoxy adhesive. When the glue has set firmly, use decorative colored tape around the bottle to conceal the joint. If you prefer, use almost any type of trim for the purpose. Lace, embossed paper, half-inch–wide anodized aluminum tape, which comes in a wide selection of colors, all make handsome, useful decorations.

SMALL URN   *Project 30*

Look for bottles of a very unusual shape. The one illustrated is a fancy liquor bottle.

Make the cut about two inches above the point where the glass sides begin to narrow, but don't attempt this as your first project; a cut like this is a little tricky and is best attempted after you've gained experience.

SIDE PLANTER *Project 31*

A catsup bottle is used for this small side planter.

This project requires only the oval cut indicated, which isn't as simple as it looks. Carefully follow the instructions given in Chapter III for the technique of cutting oval sections out of the sides of bottles.

Seal a cork into the mouth of the bottle with clear epoxy. Four almost invisible dabs of clear epoxy opposite the oval cut will provide tiny "feet" which prevent the planter from rolling or tipping over on a flat surface.

TOOTHPICK HOLDERS *Project 32*

Use almost any small bottles for this project and make the cuts about two inches above the bottom of the bottles.

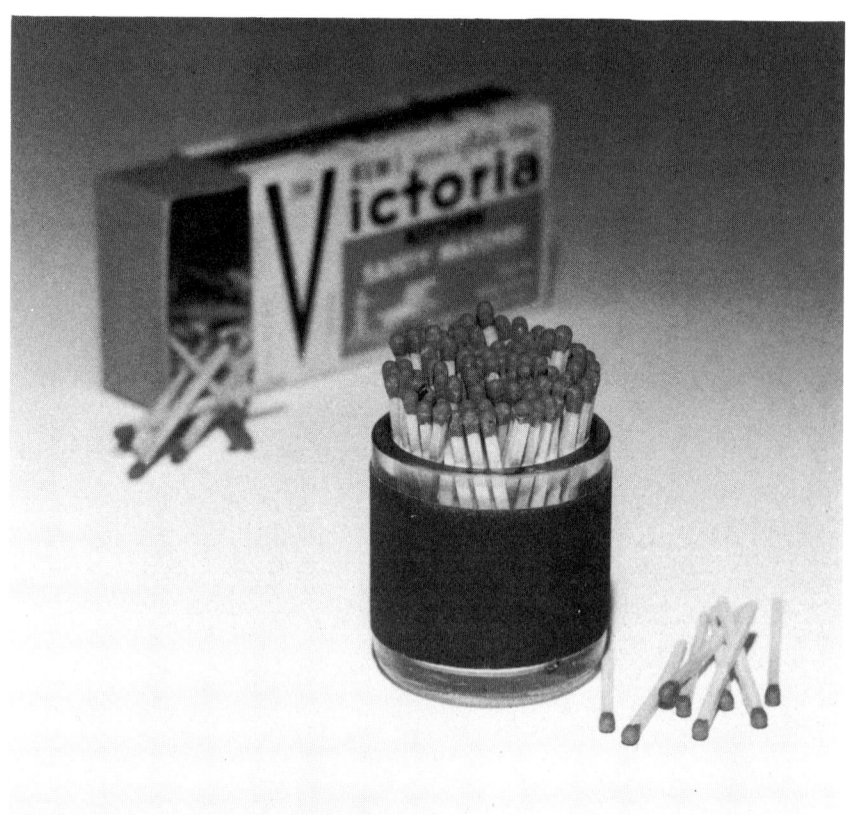

MATCH CONTAINER   Project 33

A returnable ten-ounce soda bottle is perfect for this project, as is almost any other small-diameter bottle with thick glass sides.

Make the cut about two inches above the bottom of the bottle; cut a strip of #220 emery cloth about an inch and three-quarters wide; then, using silicone adhesive, glue it around the match container, with the emery side out. Use strike-anywhere matches to fill the container. This project will be greatly appreciated where the household contains a pipe smoker. It's also a boon in the kitchen where the stove has to be lit by hand.

KEROSENE LAMP *Project 34*

For this project you'll need a long-necked wine bottle as well as another bottle of the same diameter.

Fittings for kerosene lamp wickholders vary in size, so buy your wickholder before cutting the base bottle, which should be scored so that a small stub remains after you've snapped off the neck. Fasten the threaded section of the wickholder to the projecting stub with epoxy glue; screw on the other section of the wickholder after the epoxy has completely set.

The lampshade is a straight cylinder made out of a clear glass bottle by cutting off the bottom and making another cut about six inches from the first cut. This project is easier than it sounds, and the handsome, practical lamp you make becomes invaluable when there's a power failure or when a fuse blows and you don't have a replacement.

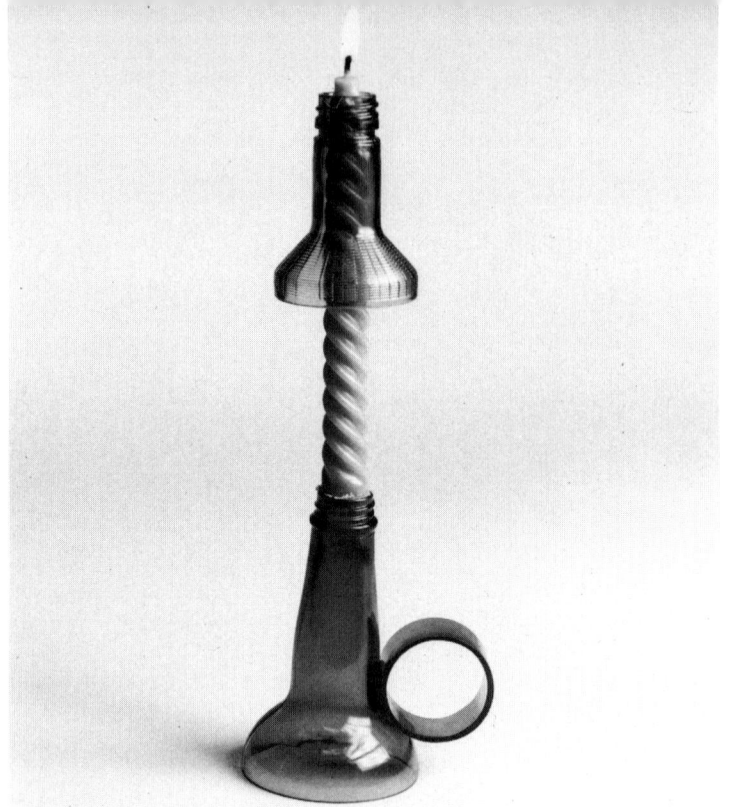

CANDLEHOLDER *Project 35*

To make this ingenious candleholder, you'll need a straight-necked wine bottle and a Bromo-Seltzer bottle.

Make the cut in the wine bottle right at the point where the tapered neck joins the straight sides. Make two cuts in the Bromo-Seltzer bottle to get a ring of blue glass one inch wide. The candle crown is cut from a whisky-sour-mix bottle at the point where the decorative trim around the neck ends.

Fasten the glass ring to the candleholder base with epoxy glue. The unique feature of this candleholder is that the candle crown rides slowly down as the candle burns. It not only adds a decorative touch but also makes the candle burn slowly and more evenly without dripping.

CANDLEHOLDERS *Projects 36 and 37*

Wine bottles are used to make these two candleholders.

For the candlestick on the left, make the cut at the point where the tapered neck joins the straight sides of the bottle.

For the candlestick on the right, make the cut just underneath the decorative trim around the top of the bottle; then, using epoxy glue, attach this bottle-neck portion to a piece cut from the bottom of a colored-glass bottle (this bottom piece should be between one-half and three-quarters of an inch high).

ASSORTED CANDLEHOLDERS

Projects 38, 39, and 40

Here are three types of candleholders, each quite different in shape and appearance, but all are made from readily available wine, beer, and soda bottles.

For the one on the left, cut the top off a nonreturnable beer bottle just below the beginning of the decorative trim.

For the one on the right, cut off the mouth of a straight-necked wine bottle; make a second cut at the point where the tapered portion at the top meets the straight sides; make a third cut about a half-inch from the bottom, then fasten the top and bottom sections together with epoxy glue.

The interesting windproof candleholder in the center is made from a scoop (see instructions for Project 21) fastened to a base made from the top section of a nonreturnable soda bottle, again using epoxy glue.

WINDPROOF CANDLESTICK Project 41

For this project you'll need three different wine and liquor bottles.

The base of the candlestick is formed from a wine bottle cut off where the tapered neck meets the straight sides. The part that actually holds the candle should be cut about four inches below the neck of the second bottle—where its diameter is at least a half inch less than the diameter of the cover (see the illustration). Fasten the two neck sections together by forcing them to share a cork, reinforcing the point where glass meets glass with epoxy glue.

The dark-colored cover is formed by cutting a Harvey's Bristol Cream or similarly shaped bottle approximately four inches from the top. The cover merely rests lightly on top of the candleholding section.

CLOCK *Project 42*

A Welch's grape-juice bottle and assorted wine bottles are needed for this modern construction.

First go through the bottles you already have on hand to find one slightly larger in circumference than the electric clock you intend to use. To form a cylindrical section slightly longer than the depth of your clock (measuring from the front of your clock to the back), make two cuts in the bottle you've chosen to hold the clock.

Grape-juice bottles have an indented finger-grip section; cut through the glass one-half inch on either side of this grip section. Next, cut three rings one to two inches wide.

Epoxy the bottle sections together as shown; when they're firmly set, fit your clock into the center glass portion and hold it in place with epoxy glue. The illustrated half-circle beneath the clock is optional.

BOTTLE-ART MOBILE *Project 43*

Nonreturnable beer bottles were used for the illustration. However, since this is a nonfunctional project—it's only purpose is to please the eye—you can use any bottles that you feel will result in an artistically satisfying mobile.

Alexander Calder, who invented the mobile, has received thousands of dollars from museums and collectors for mobiles in no way esthetically superior. By using identifiable bottle tops your finished mobile will be an example of pop art. Here is a project where only your individual taste and imagination limits the choice of bottles to employ.

To construct the mobile in the illustration, cut six nonreturnable beer bottles just at the point where the curved neck meets the straight sides. Form double hooks out of coat-hanger wire to support the bottle necks as shown; string them together in mobile fashion so that they'll bob and jiggle with air currents, using different-colored string to connect the various components.

KNICKKNACK CLUSTER Project 44

This project necessitates various types and sizes of clear and colored bottles.

Cut the bottles to the same height (about six inches from the bottom, depending on how much you want them to hold) and fasten the various glass segments together with epoxy glue, either as shown or in any combination pleasing to you.

You may want to increase the number of receptacles; if so, simply increase the number of bottles. Or you may want to limit the project to the three similar-size bottles forming the triangular cluster on the left. This is another project which you can vary and adapt to your needs and individual taste.

HOURGLASS   Project 45

You'll need two nonreturnable beer bottles or two matching bottles of almost any other type that have a nice, even taper to the neck section. Make the cuts one and a half inches below the point where the curved neck portion meets the straight sides of the bottles.

In this project don't throw away the metal screw tops; fasten them together with epoxy glue (top to top, threaded sections facing out). When the epoxy has dried completely, drill tiny holes for the sand to run through, then screw a bottle neck tightly into each top.

Cut two circular pieces of wood slightly larger than the open ends of the bottle necks. Position one of the open ends in the center of one of the wooden disks and fasten them together with epoxy glue. When they've completely dried, measure out the proper amount of clean, dry, white sand and add it to the half completed hourglass. Fasten the other disk to the open end of the other bottle with epoxy, being sure all the sand is in the bottom bottle before you begin. Sand disks smooth and stain them to taste. The three straight lengths of coat-hanger wire connect the two wooden sections. Incidentally, they are for appearance only. Use liquid metal to cover the screw tops.

DOLL *Project 46*

For this standing doll, use a beer bottle or any other bottle with a tapering neck, depending on how tall you want the doll to stand.

Make the cut at the point where the neck joins the main section of the bottle. Paint the dress on with special glass paint, and use a black-painted cork from an Almadén bottle for the head, with the doll's features marked in white. Make the hair from ten strands of yellow wool tied in the center with another strand of yellow wool and braided softly.

DOORKNOB   *Project 47*

Use a Seven-Up bottle or any other bottle with a short neck.

Make the first cut an inch from the bottom and the second cut at the point where the tapered neck joins the straight sides of the bottle. Eliminate the middle section and fasten the top and bottom sections together with epoxy glue. After the glue has hardened, fill the shortened bottle with crushed glass or aquarium stones. Fasten the knob to a door spindle with a liberal amount of epoxy glue.

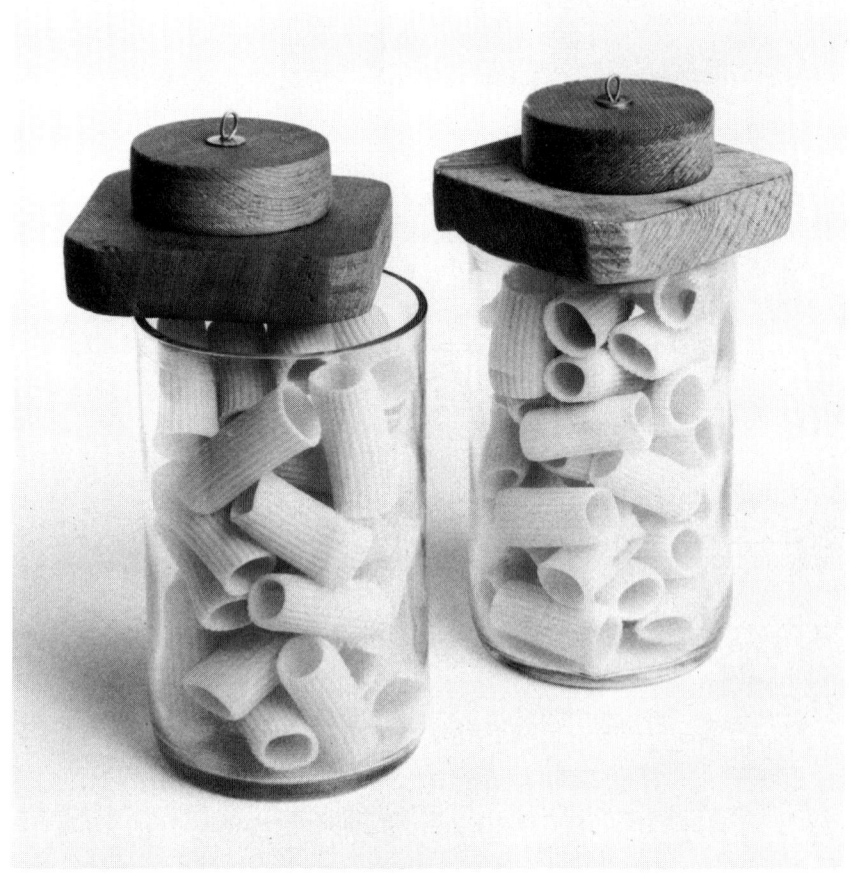

CANISTERS *Project 48*

Use clear soda bottles or any other clear bottles of similar size.

Cut the bottles right at the point where the rounded neck meets the straight sides of the bottles. Cut wooden tops large enough to slightly overlap the glass, then groove the underside of the bottom piece of the wood tops to fit the open end of the glass. Sand the wood smooth, join the two pieces with a cotter pin and washer as shown, stain them, and apply any clear finish after the stain has thoroughly dried.

MEASURING CUPS Project 49

Use almost any kind of small lightweight bottles. Four small bottles of different sizes are needed for this project.

Carefully measure out the exact amount of liquid that each measuring cup is to contain, such as one ounce, four ounces, or what is handiest for you, then mark each bottle at that point, and cut each one where marked. Carefully wrap some coat-hanger wire around each glass and extend it out into a short handle, then apply two coats of liquid metal to achieve the rugged effect shown.

WISHING WELL *Project 50*

A wine bottle or any similar type of tinted bottle is used for this project. Cut two four-inch sections from the straight center portion of the bottle, then cut one of the sections in half with a handcutter to form two half-circles.

The upright sections are made of two pieces of wood fastened to the inside of the glass circle with epoxy glue. Before gluing, drill holes in the wood for the crank, which is formed of coat-hanger wire.

The bottle cap forms the bucket. Drill holes in the bottle cap and string it to the crank as shown in the illustration. Glue one of the half-circles of glass to the top of the wooden supports to form the roof.

WATER PIPE   *Project 51*

For the body of the pipe, use any short-necked wine bottle. Make two cuts, the first a half-inch from the bottom, the second a half-inch from the point where the rounded neck joins the straight sides of the bottle. After you've smoothed the two cut edges, join them with epoxy glue.

The bowl and the stem of the pipe come from a chemical supply house; so does the rubber cork. The bowl is called a thistle tube and must be cut so that the stem, when pushed through the cork, will clear the bottom of the glass container by about half an inch. The rest of the tube is cut off and bent over a flame; then fitted through the second hole in the cork.

BATHROOM RACK *Project 52*

You'll need three matching wine bottles for this interesting project. Make the cuts about four and a half inches from the bottom of the bottles.

Cut a piece of wood about eleven inches long and slightly wider than the diameter of the bottles. Sand the wood smooth, stain it, and apply several coats of clear lacquer or varnish. Fasten the bottom of the bottles to the wood with epoxy, centering them carefully. Add a sturdy, decorative hanger at the top of the wood.

WALL KNICKKNACK RACK *Project 53*

Use three matching bottles of almost any type and cut the bottles approximately one inch from the bottom. Obtain a piece of wood about nine inches long and four inches wide, sand it smooth, stain it, and apply two coats of clear lacquer, then fasten the bottle bottoms to the wood with epoxy. If you have the wall space, you can attach two, three, or even four rows of bottle bottoms mounted on a larger piece of wood for a smashing effect. A strip of gold paper trim adds a nice decorative touch.

NAPKIN RINGS *Project 54*

You'll need only one bottle about one and a half inches in diameter for two, or even three, napkin rings. To make these perfectly charming items, simply make the cuts an inch apart.

CHRISTMAS ORNAMENTS *Project 55*

Here you can utilize whatever bottles you want, although it's strongly suggested that you keep them as small as possible.

For the ornament on the left, cut the tops off two beer bottles and epoxy them together; when the ornament is dry, hide the joint with gold paper trim. Next, drill a hole through a cork, run a string through the hole, and tie a large knot in the string; then, epoxy the cork into the bottle neck.

For the ornament on the right, use any bottle with an interesting shape or color and cut it as close to the bottom as is pleasing to your eye, then attach a cork and string as you did above. You can also make a charming bell out of this ornament by allowing the string to extend about three-quarters of the way into the cut bottle and by tying a metal washer to the end of the string.

PITCHER, MUG, AND DISH   *Projects 56, 57, and 58*

The pitcher is made from a Wesson oil bottle; the dish from a half-gallon milk bottle; and the mug from a wine bottle.

For the pitcher, mark off the scalloped edge of the oil bottle with a felt-tipped pen; following the outline, carefully score the glass with a handcutter; then tap the glass with particular care to remove the cut segments. Take special pains in smoothing the scalloped edges.

For the mug, cut the wine bottle six inches from the bottom; next, cut an inch-wide ring from any available bottle of a slightly larger diameter; then cut the ring in half with a handcutter to make the handle. Attach this half-circle with epoxy.

Make the dish by cutting the half-gallon milk bottle as close to the bottom as possible.

PEN OR PENCIL HOLDER *Project 59*

Use almost any colored bottle. Make the base of the holder by cutting the bottle as close to the bottom as possible. Form a tapered coil from stiff wire for the ballpoint pen or pencil to slip into easily. Attach the tapered coil to the center of the bottle bottom with epoxy.

PICTURE FRAME *Project 60*

Any type of colored bottles can be used for this unique project.

Cut as many one-inch rings as you decide to use. For the three-ring frame shown here, cut a piece of wood approximately four inches wide and ten inches long. Sand the wood smooth, stain it, then apply two coats of lacquer. Place one of the glass rings over each picture you've decided to frame; then, use the inside of the glass ring as a guide to pencil-mark the photographs; finally, cut the pictures along the marked lines.

Fasten the glass rings to the board with epoxy; when they're dry, simply insert the chosen photographs.

Depending on your wall space or chosen location, you may wish to use more rings for a larger picture-frame arrangement. If so, the backboard must be of an appropriate shape and size.

BOOK ENDS *Project 61*

Any two fairly large, matching bottles of pleasing shape and color can be used for these bottle book ends. The ones illustrated are sixteen-ounce nonreturnable Seven-Up bottles.

Cut the bottles four inches from the point where the tapered neck meets the straight sides. Cut two pieces of wood approximately four inches long and four inches wide. Sand smooth, stain, and apply any clear finish. Fasten the bottles to the wood with epoxy, making sure that the open end of each bottle is aligned with the board forming the base.

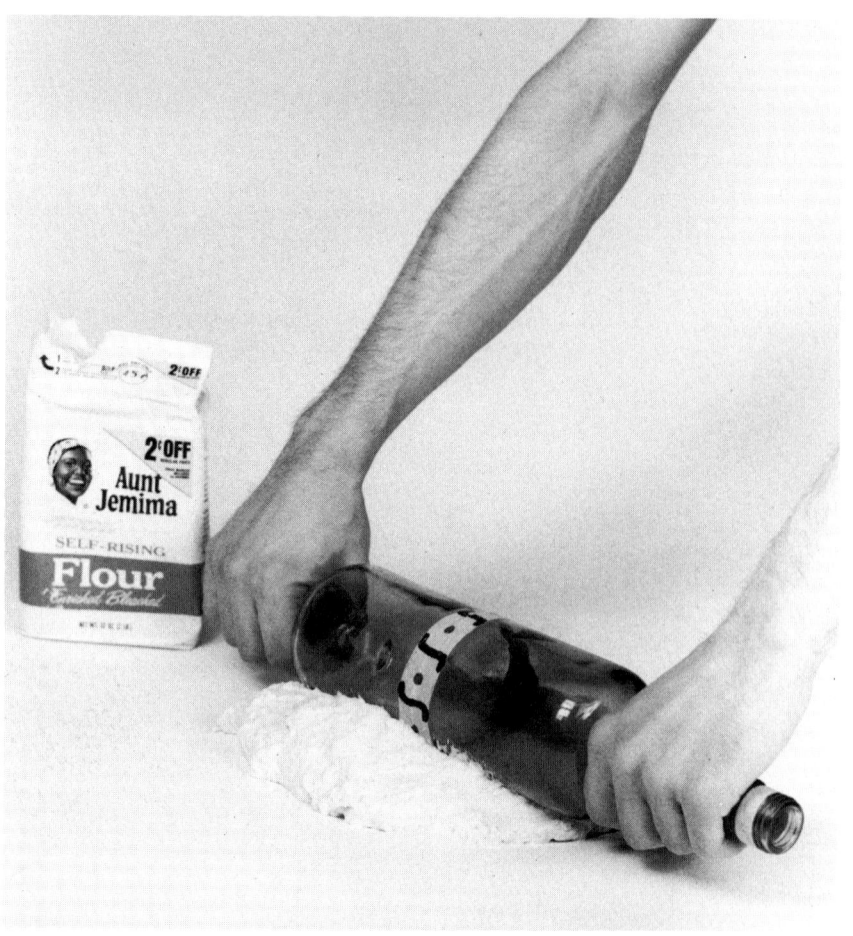

ROLLING PIN FOR DECORATION *Project 62*

Use two wine bottles. Make the cut one inch from the bottom of the bottles, then fasten the cut ends of the bottles together with epoxy. Use glass paint to form any decorative pattern you like for the handles and the center portion where the bottles are joined together. These make dandy and decorative conversation starters, but they're not recommended for rolling your pie crusts.

HORN *Project 63*

Use any bottle with a nice-looking flare at the top.

Make the cut just above the point where the neck meets the straight sides of the bottle. Fasten the noise-making element from any toy horn to the inside of the glass neck with epoxy.

PAPERWEIGHT Project 64

A Harvey's Bristol Cream bottle or any dark-colored, stubby-necked bottle can be used.

Cut the bottle approximately one inch below the point where the rounded neck meets the straight sides of the bottle. To add weight to the cut bottle, fill the inside of the cut glass wih dark-colored plaster clay or cement. If the filling shrinks and falls out after drying, allow it to harden completely, then glue it back in position with epoxy.

TERRARIUM *Project 65*

You'll need two clear-glass gallon jugs.

Cut one of the jugs four inches from the bottom. Fill the bottom section with potting soil and pot one of the many plants that thrive in a terrarium. Cut the second jug as close to the bottom as possible—just before the glass starts to curve in. The top section of the second jug should be precisely the diameter of the bottom section of the first jug. Use epoxy to seal these two segments together.

INCENSE BURNER *Project 66*

Use any type of bottle and cut an oval-shaped segment out of the side of the bottle, following the detailed instructions given in Chapter III. Fill the section below the cut with small stones or fish-tank gravel to form a bed for the incense.

BOTTLE RACK *Project 67*

Use nonreturnable quart beer bottles or any other dark-colored, large-size bottles. Make the cuts just below the point where the curved neck section meets the straight sides of the bottle. Epoxy the cut bottles together along their sides to form a square three bottles by three bottles.

Cut two strips of wood fourteen and a half inches long and two strips eight inches long. All four pieces should be about an inch and a half wide. Smooth, stain, and finish the wood. Nail the short pieces to the long pieces at right angles. Finally, use epoxy to fasten the bottom row of bottles to the finished boards.

CIGARETTE CONTAINER *Project 68*

You'll need two wine bottles, one of a slightly larger diameter than the other.

Cut the smaller bottle four inches from the bottom. Cut the larger bottle exactly as you did the scoop in Project 21. Glue an attractive cap onto the mouth of the larger bottle, and assemble the two parts as shown. They should make a reasonably good fit to keep the tobacco fresh.

EGG TIMER AND EGG CUP *Projects 69 and 70*

Use two small whisky bottles of the airline type for the egg timer and cut them as close to the bottom as possible. Fasten the outside of the two bottle tops together with epoxy. When the epoxy has set firmly, drill a one-sixteenth–inch hole through both tops. Cut two one-and-a-quarter–inch squares of plywood, sand them, and stain them. After adding sand, fasten the bases to the bottle bottoms. If you wish, fasten gold foil around the caps with silicone adhesive.

Use a Guinness stout bottle and a Piels beer bottle for the egg cup. Cut the Guinness bottle five inches from the top. Cut the beer bottle at the point where the rounded neck joins the straight sides of the bottle. Fasten the bottle necks together with epoxy. After the epoxy has hardened, use silicone adhesive to add either gold or other colored paper trim around both the neck and the bottom of the base bottle.

HOT-POT   *Projects 71 and 72*
TRIVET AND LADLE

For the trivet, cut nine matching wine bottles three-quarters of an inch from the bottom. Obtain an eight-inch–square piece of plywood; sand, stain, and finish it. Attach the inverted bottle bottoms to the finished wood base with epoxy. If you want to add a decorative touch, attach any kind of cutout or picture to the inside of the bottle bottoms before affixing them to the base.

   For the ladle, use a wine bottle or almost any other bottle of similar shape and attractive color.

   Make the cut three inches from the bottom of the bottle. For the handle, use two lengths of twisted coat-hanger wire fitted into a wooden handle if you don't have a discarded handle from an old kitchen set. Attach the wire handle to the side of the bottle bottom with metallic-colored epoxy. Smooth the epoxy into a nice even shape. To make sure of a good bond, slightly roughen the glass surface at the point where the wire is to be attached.

SALT AND PEPPER CELLARS *Project 73*

This project calls for two eight-ounce Coca-Cola bottles or two other bottles of a similar size and with an attractive pattern in the glass. Cut the bottles approximately two inches from the bottom. You'll also need two small, gracefully bent, ladle-type spoons to complete this interesting project.

GOLD-TRIMMED GLASSES AND FOOTED GOLD-TRIMMED GLASSES

Projects 74 and 75

Use any colored beer bottles to make these decorative glasses. Make the cuts four, five, or six inches from the bottom of the bottle and use silicone adhesive to fasten decorative gold paper trim to the outside of the glasses. When the adhesive is thoroughly dry, apply two or three coats of decoupage varnish to protect the trim. Despite the protective coating, carefully wash the finished glasses by hand after using them.

For the footed glasses, nonreturnable dark-brown beer bottles are excellent. For the top section of the glasses, make the cuts four, five, or six inches from the bottom of the bottles. For the bases, make the cuts at the point where the neck joins the straight sides of the bottles. Affix the bases to the top sections with epoxy. When the epoxy is thoroughly dry, fasten gold-foil trim to the glasses with silicone adhesive; when this is thoroughly dry, brush on several coats of decoupage varnish to protect the delicate paper coating. Continue to protect the paper by washing the glasses very gently after using them.

LACE-TRIMMED GLASSES *Project 76*

Here you can use almost any kind of bottle and cut it where you feel the proportions of the given bottle are the most pleasing to your eye and the most practical for your intended use. After you've made the glasses from the bottles by the appropriate cuts, buy inexpensive lace trim, which is available at the notions counter of department stores, dime stores, or millinery stores. Fasten the trim to the glasses with silicone adhesive; when the adhesive is dry, coat the trim with several coats of decoupage varnish. Wash glasses gently, swiftly, and carefully after using them.

CAKE COVER *Project 77*

Use a clear gallon jug and a miniature whisky bottle to make this handsome cake cover. Cut the jug ten inches from the bottom. Make the handle from a miniature airline-type whisky bottle. Cut the small bottle an inch and a half from the bottom. Using epoxy glue, fasten the open end of the small bottle to the center of the jug bottom.

WOOL HOLDER

Project 78

You'll need any two bottles of similar size and color.

Cut the base bottle two and a half inches from the bottom. Cut the second bottle, which must be exactly the same diameter as the base bottle, one inch below the point where the curved neck meets the straight sides. Buy a small strip of thin brass trim at a hardware or cabinet-supply store, then fasten it around the rim of the bottom bottle with clear epoxy so that one-half the width of the brass trim projects above the glass. This forms a guide to hold the top half in perfect alignment.

When the project is finished, drop a ball of yarn inside the bottom bottle, then feed the end of the yarn through the neck of the upper bottle.

INKWELL *Project 79*

Use a nail-polish bottle for this project and make the cut about an inch and a half from the bottom of the bottle. Be careful cutting this type of bottle—the glass tends to snap irregularly.

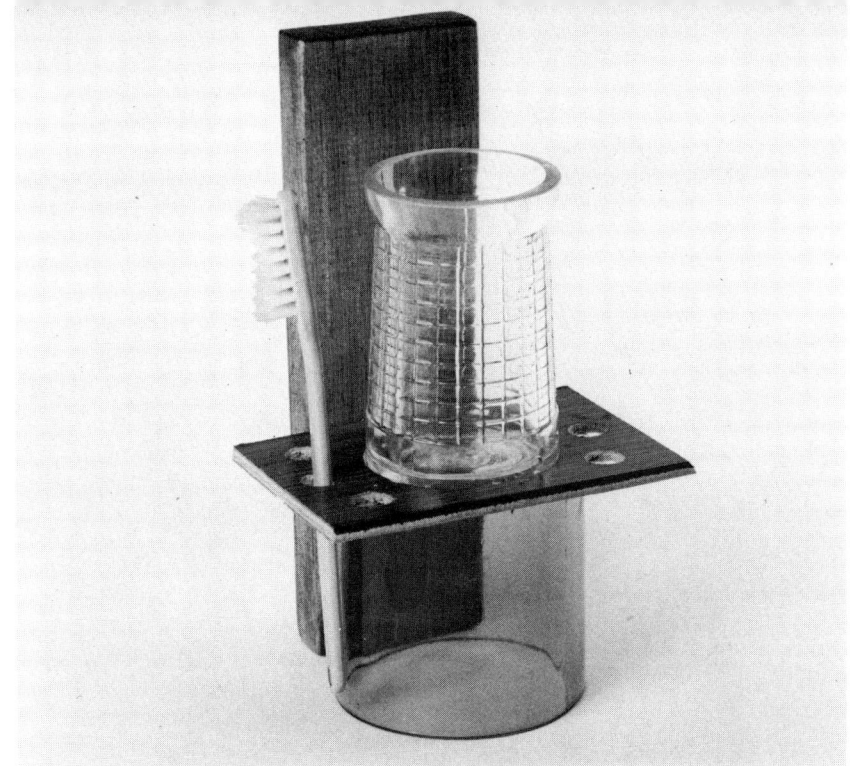

TOOTHBRUSH HOLDER AND BATHROOM GLASS

Projects 80 and 81

For these projects, use a wine bottle and a small Canada Dry bottle. For the base of the toothbrush holder, cut off the bottom of the wine bottle, then make a second cut four inches above the first cut so that you have a straight-sided, four-inch cylinder. Make the bathroom glass by cutting the small Canada Dry bottle just above the design.

For the stand, cut a piece of thin wood eight inches long and three and a half inches wide; sand, stain, and finish the wood with clear coating. Fasten the large-diameter glass cylinder to the wood with clear epoxy glue. Cut a second piece of wood four inches square and drill six half-inch holes on two sides plus a two-inch hole in the center. Sand, stain, and finish the wood. Fasten it to the top of the glass cylinder with clear epoxy.

COASTER *Project 82*

Use almost any bottle of the right size to make this coaster. Simply cut the bottle as close to the bottom as possible.

SALT AND PEPPER SHAKERS *Project 83*

Two small, matching medicine bottles are ideal for this project. Cut the bottles about two inches from the bottom. Cut two circles of thin aluminum (the bottoms of aluminum soft-drink or beer cans are excellent) so that they are about a quarter of an inch larger than the outside diameter of the glass; drill a series of small holes in the aluminum tops; then make a series of wedge-shaped cuts around the overhanging portion of the rims; finally, bend the overhang down so that it cups the sides of the glass. Brass gallery trim, fixed over the aluminum overhang with epoxy adhesive, will hide any irregularities.

SNACK DISH CLUSTER *Project 84*

Use straight-sided bottles for this project. While you can use any size bottle you wish, be sure to cut all the bottles to the same height—about seven inches from the bottom. Fasten the sides together with epoxy, in any configuration pleasing to you. This is a superb party item that keeps all the dry snacks together in one place.

HURRICANE LAMP *Project 85*

You'll need a champagne bottle (or any other bottle with a bell, or dimple, in the bottom) and a straight-sided wine bottle of a slightly larger diameter to fit over the first bottle.

Cut the champagne bottle two inches from the bottom, then cut the wine bottle as close to the bottom as possible, making a second cut in the wine bottle just below the point where the curved neck section meets the straight sides of the bottle. These two cuts give you a tall, straight-sided cylinder.

Cut three small pieces of wood, stain them, and finish them. Fasten them with epoxy to the bottom of the cylinder so that the cylinder is raised an inch above the table. The bottom of the champagne bottle turned upside down forms the candleholder, and the glass cylinder fitted over it acts as a windscreen. (Instructions for the match container are given in Project 33.)

CANDLEHOLDER AND WIND CHIMES

Projects 86 and 87

Use beer bottles for both of these projects. For the candleholder, cut one of the beer bottles about three inches from the bottom. For the base of the candleholder, cut another beer bottle about four inches from the bottom.

Cut two pieces of wood, the first eight inches long and four inches wide, the second a square the same diameter as the base of the bottle; sand, stain, and finish both pieces of wood; then nail or screw the small wooden square to the larger piece.

Attach the three-inch candleholder to the backboard with epoxy; then attach the four-inch base to the small wooden square with epoxy. Decorate the base with metallic paper trim held in place with silicone adhesive; when the adhesive is dry, protect the paper with two or three coats of decoupage varnish. Use a stubby, large-diameter candle or fill the candleholder with melted wax and insert a wick before it hardens.

Make the wind chimes from nonreturnable beer bottles or from any other pleasantly shaped bottles. Cut them just below the point where the straight sides begin.

Push strong, thin string, such as nylon or filament fishline, through a cork. Tie a small metal washer to one end of the string and pull the string through the cork. The string should be just long enough so that the metal washer makes a nice ringing sound when it hits the inside of the bottle. Force the cork in place and secure it with a small amount of epoxy. Make a loop in the other end of the string and attach it to a long hook fastened to either end of the backboard. Hang the unit outside for flickering candlelight and a gentle, tinkling sound from every breeze.

SMALL DESKLAMP *Project 88*

This lamp is made from a long-necked wine bottle and a dark, short, wide bottle, such as a port-wine, Drambuie, or Harvey's Bristol Cream bottle.

Cut the wine bottle two inches below the point where the rounded neck meets the straight sides. Cut the darker bottle that forms the lampshade an inch below the point where the rounded neck section meets the straight sides. Fasten the shade to the top of the wine-bottle base with epoxy.

Use metallic paper trim around the bottom of the shade and use lace or lace paper around the neck. Use silicone adhesive to attach the decoration and apply decoupage varnish to protect it.

Drill a hole through a cork, then wire a small lamp socket and run the lampcord up through the hole in the cork, which fits into the top bottle neck. Secure the cork with a small amount of epoxy glue.

SHOT GLASSES   Project 89

Use miniature, airline-type whisky bottles and calibrate each shot glass by measuring out the exact amount of liquid you want it to hold, pouring it into the bottle, and marking the liquid level. Cut the bottles at this point.

SHAVING DISH *Project 90*

Two clear, nonreturnable quart soda bottles are good for both the shaving dish and the cover.

For the shaving dish, cut one soda bottle two and three-quarter inches from the bottom; for the lid, cut the other bottle about three-quarters of an inch from the bottom. Substituting dark-colored bottles of the same size results in a practical and handsome denture cup.

INCENSE-STICK BURNER *Project 91*

A nonreturnable Seven-Up bottle, a wine bottle, and a cork are the materials needed for this special item. Cut the Seven-Up bottle at the point where the rounded neck meets the straight sides. Cut the wine bottle about three-quarters of an inch from the bottom.

Drill two or three small holes in the cork, then fasten the cork into the mouth of the bottle with a small amount of epoxy glue. The ends of the incense-sticks fit into the holes, while the wine-bottle bottom forms the base and makes a nice color contrast.

HANGING LAMP   *Project 92*

The bottle part of this ambitious project consists of four nonreturnable Seven-Up bottles or four similarly shaped bottles with screw tops. Make the cuts about three-quarters of an inch from the bottom of the bottles.

Cut two pieces of wood sixteen inches long and about an inch and a half wide; notch them in the center so that they fit together to form a cross.

Drill quarter-inch holes in the screw caps of the soda bottles and matching holes in the ends of each of the four wood pieces. Fasten the bottle caps down with epoxy glue, lining up the holes carefully. Wire up four small sockets. Feed the wire down through the bottles and the wood pieces. Run all four cords to the center of the wooden cross; fasten a metal can securely to the exact center of the upper side of the wood, using epoxy glue and wood screws. Drill a half-inch hole through the can and the wood strips underneath. Feed the wires up through this hole into the can; connect them together and continue a single length of wire upward into an electrical outlet. Drill four holes in the side of the can, attach leather thongs, and bring them together at a point about ten inches above the can. Braid the leather thongs and the wire together and attach both to a hook in the ceiling or a supporting chain, but make sure that the strain is carried by the leather thongs and not by the electric wire. Use small-voltage bulbs for the best effect.

The wooden part of this project looks much better dark. If the wood is stained, use dark stain and paint the tin can a very dark brown. Black paint for wood and tin can is also effective.

WHISTLE *Project 93*

To make this whistle, you can use almost any type of bottle with a long neck.

Cut the bottle at the point where the neck joins the wide portion of the bottle. Fashion a wooden whistle like the one shown in the illustration or buy a wood or metal whistle in a dime store or toy shop and fit it into the mouth of the bottle with epoxy. The glass will act as a resonator.

LARGE FLOWER VASE
Project 94

For this project you'll need a very large bottle called a jeroboam. Twice the size of a magnum, it's usually used for champagne. If you're a millionaire, you can order a jeroboam of champagne just to get the bottle. A better way is to call your neighborhood liquor dealers to find out if they sell jeroboams; if any of them do, ask them to call you whenever they sell one, to tell you who bought it. They're often sold in large numbers for weddings and coming-out parties. Rather than waiting for the garbage, call the purchaser and ask him to save the bottles for you. If you can't find a jeroboam, you may be fortunate enough to find another bottle of similar dimensions.

When you find your jeroboam, simply cut off the neck where it joins the straight sides and you'll have a vase that would cost you many dollars at any fine shop.

INDIVIDUAL FLOWER CONTAINERS
Project 95

Use flat, miniature liquor bottles or any small bottles of the same shape. Cut the bottles just below the neck to give straight-sided containers. They are very effective grouped together around a larger piece and make handsome individual flower containers for a formal dinner-place setting.

HANGING CONTAINER FOR IVY
Project 96

Use pint or half-pint flat-flask liquor bottles. Make the cuts just below the point where the shoulders of the bottles meet the straight sides. Drill four holes for the hanging cords. (See Chapter III for details on drilling holes in glass.)

Select a variety of ivy that grows in water and plant nutrient alone. Attach colorful cords and hang the container from a hook in the ceiling or from a wall bracket, allowing the ivy to droop down gracefully.

CANDLEHOLDERS
Project 97

Use champagne or sparkling-burgundy bottles or any large bottles with dimples or bell-shaped indentations in the bottom. Cut each bottle about three inches from the bottom. Melt some wax onto the dimple in the bottom of the bottle and attach a small, slender candle. Fill the bottle bottom with water and float flower petals on the surface of the water.

RAFFIA-WRAPPED FLOWER CONTAINERS
Project 98

Miniature, airline-type liquor bottles or any small bottles of a similar shape are ideal for this purpose.

Don't cut the bottles for this project. Simply soak off the labels and group the bottles together, then wrap brightly colored straw raffia around the bottles and spray the raffia with clear plastic to protect it. Very carefully select the individual flowers you're going to use, and cut the stems to different lengths for a charming display.

CIGARETTE AND FLOWER HOLDERS
Project 99

You'll need two miniature, airline-type liquor bottles, one round and one oval-shaped; make sure both are straight-sided. Cut them about three inches from the bottom and glue them together with epoxy. When they're dry, wrap them with raffia or colored string, then brush or spray the raffia with plastic to protect the covering.

Partially fill one of the bottles with water and float a few tiny flowers on the water, then put two or three cigarettes into the matching container, and you have a perfect addition to any table setting.

Projects 94, 95, 96, 97, 98, and 99

PERSONALIZED PRETZEL BOWL AND STRAW-AND-STIRRER HOLDER

Projects 100 and 101

For the pretzel bowl, use a dark-colored wine bottle or any similar dark bottle. Cut the bottle just below the point where the rounded neck portion meets the straight sides. Use glass paint in a contrasting color to inscribe the names of your friends or neighbors.

For the holder, use flask-type whisky bottles or any similarly shaped bottles. Cut the bottles just below the point where the rounded neck portion meets the straight sides. Fasten the flat sides of the bottles together with epoxy; when the epoxy has set, wrap the bottles with brightly colored twine. Brush or spray a coat of clear plastic on the twine to protect it from stains.

PERSONALIZED GLASSES Project 102

Use almost any type clear-glass bottles to make these individualized glasses.

Make the cuts to result in whatever size tumblers you desire or in the appropriate size for your friends' favorite drinks. Use glass paint to write the names of your friends and their favorite drinks right on their special glasses. This is not only a very warm way of saying welcome when your friends visit you, but it also saves time and confusion for the host or hostess.

SPEAKER BOTTLE *Project 103*

Use a one-gallon jug for this unusual piece of audio equipment. Cut the jug two inches from the bottom, then bend a supporting rack out of coat-hanger wire to suspend the speakers inside the bottle.

WITHDRAWN
By
Peter White Public Library

000 627 49⸱

for bottle cutters.

DATE DUE			
JUL 1973 6			
SEP 18 1973			
JAN 1974 4			
JAN 1974 16			
FEB 1974 20			
JUL 1974 3			
OCT 9 1974			
Jan 29 '75			
May 7 '75			
May 21 '75			
Apr 7 '76			
Oct 27 '76			
Nov 18 '81			
Feb 8 '04			
JUN 24 '87			
GAYLORD			PRINTED IN U.S.A.